C000294197

INTERNATIONAL
GARDEN
PHOTOGRAPHER OF THE YEAR

COLLECTION 02

Managing Editor: Paul Mitchell
Senior Art Editor: Nick Otway
Senior Editor: Donna Wood
Image retouching and colour repro: Sarah Montgomery
Indexer: Hilary Bird

Produced by AA Publishing
© AA Media Limited 2009

Published by AA Publishing (a trading name of AA Media Limited, whose registered
office is Fanum House, Basing View, Basingstoke, Hampshire RG21 4EA;
registered number 06112600)

A4064
ISBN: 978-0-7495-6182-6

A CIP catalogue record for this book is available from the British Library.

Printed and bound in the UK by Butler Tanner & Dennis

theAA.com/bookshop

HEATHER EDWARDS ···⟩   Finalist

The secret garden.
The Old Malthouse, Wiltshire, England.

A mown path leads through a sea of cow parsley (*Anthriscus sylvestris*) to a willow (*Salix*)
arch on a still, early, summer morning. This part of the garden was in complete contrast to
the rest of the garden, which was more formal and well maintained. I felt my eyes drawn
into the cow parsley by the mown path and could imagine this setting in a children's story,
perhaps leading to a secret garden.

3

CONTENTS

⚘ PAUL DEBOIS   Finalist

Gregg Wallace.
The orchards at Brogdale, Kent, England.
Art Direction Abigail Dodd.

Food expert Gregg Wallace in the orchard at Brogdale. Illustrating an article on Apples in BBC *Gardeners' World*
magazine, I was briefed to capture his humour using the William Tell theme. At the same time, the photograph had
to capture the atmosphere of a late summer orchard. The apples in the background and the one on Gregg's head
were chosen for their colour, not variety. Whenever you take a celebrity portrait, you're usually on a strict deadline
and often don't know what to expect from a session. In this instance, Gregg was the perfect sitter and the photos
almost took themselves – we just had to hope the camera motordrive could keep up with his quick-fire humour!

FOREWORD

by Chris Beardshaw

The transient and ephemeral nature of a garden with its diverse ingredients of light, subject, time, season and weather is a mercurial thing, sometimes frustratingly complex to absorb. The drama, theatre and energy present create a unique experience for viewers – one that moves those with an assumed level of understanding while avoiding exclusion of those new to the subject. It has the power to provoke tears of frustration but create balance with tears of joy. It caresses, cavorts with and challenges our senses, engaging hearts and minds. It demands our attention while stimulating self-analysis but is also capable of appearing as an apparently benign backdrop to our lives.

Social statements, sculptural exploration, personal expression and whimsical fantasies may all be evident and then, of course, there is that most valuable of ingredients; untamed nature. From insects to sociable mammals, single-celled algae to complex fungi – all provide additional enlivening ingredients in the creation of an enthralling and intimate experience.

Capturing this most intricate of multifaceted sculptures is a challenge for garden photographers. For me, the ability to harness and portray such a garden is every bit as complex as its initial creation. Truly great photographs are more than records of a single moment in time but are capable of transporting their viewer, placing them as a player on the garden stage. It is for precisely this reason that this book is a privilege to experience. Packed with a selection of tempting and tantalising works of art it demonstrates that, in the hands of an artist, the familiar can appear magical and the magical can become iconic. This book also demonstrates that the profession of photography is more vibrant than ever and that those practising it are capable of rising to any challenge that gardeners, nature and the environment may place before them.

Chris Beardshaw

PERSPECTIVE FROM THE ROYAL BOTANIC GARDENS, KEW

Professor Stephen Hopper FLS,
Director of the Royal Botanic Gardens, Kew

Kew is delighted to have hosted the exhibition on which this stunning book is based. Because 2009 is a very special year for us – our 250th anniversary – we are particularly pleased to see the category on World Botanic Gardens.

From humble beginnings as a 'physick garden', Kew has grown to include the world's most diverse collections of living and preserved plants, plant artefacts and botanical art. These resources are not only vital to the people who work in scientific endeavour and plant conservation at Kew, but also to our international partners – more than 800 in over 100 countries.

So are botanic gardens just places of study for expert botanists, horticulturists and scientists? The images in this book show that this is far from true. Botanic gardens are in fact places of beauty where both specialists and ordinary visitors can marvel and wonder at plants in their glorious, diverse richness.

At Kew we aim to provide our visitors with inspiring experiences. We hope to delight and help them to discover more about plants and how they interact in their surrounding environment. We also want to encourage people to think about the role of plants in their own lives, and their continuing and ever-increasing importance in our changing world. Ultimately, we aim to inspire and deliver science-based plant conservation, enhancing the quality of life. By caring for plants and living sustainably with them we care for ourselves.

The images in this book reinforce these ideas – and most of all they convey the enthusiasm and imagination of talented photographers, their passion for plants and our living world.

Kew 250th

PLANTS PEOPLE POSSIBILITIES

🕈 HILARY FORSTER   CommENDED

Informal vegetable-growing.
Turmstrasse, Tiergarten, Berlin, Germany.

I loved this brilliantly inventive and opportunistic garden, located in the heart of Berlin.
A local resident had constructed a deep bed in a space normally occupied by a tree. The
sides of the bed were made from recycled orange boxes, carefully joined to produce a neat
enclosure. The plants were pest-free and marigolds were used as companion plants to the
corn, herbs and salad ingredients. It was wonderful to see vegetables growing and lovingly
tended in the heart of the city.

THE ORGANISERS

INTERNATIONAL GARDEN PHOTOGRAPHER OF THE YEAR

International Garden Photographer of the Year is run by Garden and Landscape Photographic Arts Ltd.

The four directors of the UK-based company are Philip Smith, Jane Nichols, Andrew Lawson and Clive Nichols.

The competition and exhibition are organised by Philip Smith, assisted by Mary Denton.

Thanks

International Garden Photographer of the Year would like to thank the following for their practical help with the competition and exhibition.

Special thanks to Mic Cady for helping us bring this book to life in the first place.

Thanks to all the judges who gave up their time to help us come to a series of very difficult decisions.

- For the Royal Botanic Gardens, Kew: David Yard and the marketing team, the Estates team, the Press Office.
- For the AA: David Watchus, Ian Little, Nick Otway, Sarah Montgomery, Paul Mitchell.
- For the National Trust: Karen Bolger, Roger Watson, Sue Carter, Chris Lacey, Victoria Skeet.
- For Standard 8: Matt Haycocks and all the team.
- For Little Green Monkey: Hagar Lee, Ben Waterson.
- For the Royal Photographic Society: Liz Williams.
- For *Bises* Inc: Japan: Hanako Yagi.
- For BGCI: Per Bogstad, Julia Willison, Sara Oldfield, Suzanne Sharrock.

For their invaluable individual help and support: Eddie Ephraums, Julie Kelly, Briony Lawson, Eileen Powell, Hannah and Elsie Powell-Smith, Hannah Whitworth, Kerry Banner, Ailsa McWhinnie, Val Bourne, Susie Pickering.

Above all, the whole International Garden Photographer of the Year team thanks all the photographers who have entered the competition. Whether selected or not, their photographs have been a joy to review, a privilege to share and an inspiration to all.

BISES Inc. Japan

For over twenty-five years, Hanako Yagi has been editor-in-chief of some of Japan's leading handicraft and interior design magazines. These magazines opened up new worlds and strongly influenced the leisure activities of Japanese people. A fortuitous meeting on her very first visit to England led her to discover the rich and stimulating world of English-style 'flower' gardening. She

found English gardens to be the polar opposite of traditional Japanese gardens which have a style established by many centuries. In 1992, she launched *BISES*, Japan's first home and garden magazine. The magazine pioneered and spread floral gardening in Japan and created a new lifestyle that men and women of all ages could enjoy. *BISES* is well known for its high-quality photography, editing style and reproduction. Hanako kindly judged the *Spirit of the Japanese Garden* special award.
Hanako Yagi, Guest Judge

The Royal Photographic Society

The Royal Photographic Society was founded in 1853 'to promote the Art and Science of Photography', a mission it continues to this day in the United Kingdom and through its considerable overseas membership.

Awards

Photographers from all over the world were invited to enter single images or themed portfolios in any of the competition categories.

International Garden Photographer of the Year was awarded to the best single image.

Best Portfolio award was given to the best themed portfolio.

Runner-up prizes were awarded to the portfolios judged second and third.

A first, second and third award was given for each competition category.

In addition, a number of photographs in each category were judged to be 'Finalist'.

These finalist and winner photographs form the International Garden Photographer of the Year exhibition at the Royal Botanic Gardens, Kew and other venues.

A number of photographs were also selected as 'Commended' in each category. These appear on our website and are also published in this book.

Special Awards:
- Young International Garden Photographer of the Year for under 16s only.
- Spirit of the Japanese garden – awarded by *Bises* Inc, Japan.
- GPA Best Portfolio – awarded by the Garden Photographers' Association.

Part of the Garden Writers' Guild

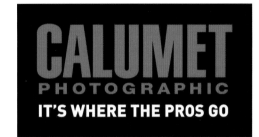

THE CATEGORIES

Garden Views

Visiting a garden is a great day out for many of us. We can stand and admire the work of gardeners who have dedicated themselves to creating a personal paradise for the enjoyment of themselves and others. Images could be submitted from gardens in any part of the world, from Tokyo to Capetown, from Glasgow to Melbourne. Photographers were invited to submit images that showed what is special about a particular garden, whether it is large or small, whether it is a chic design statement or a plantsman's paradise.

World Botanic Gardens

Botanic gardens are places of beauty, discovery and learning, where botanists, scientists, horticulturalists and educators work to nurture, conserve, and raise awareness about the world's endangered plants. This category sought to discover how botanic gardens are viewed in the 21st century. Almost every country in the world has at least one botanic garden and every garden has its own unique character.

The Edible Garden

Growing your own vegetables and fruit is more popular then ever. From carrots and cauliflowers to exotic fruits and herbs, we can all grow something to eat. The formal kitchen gardens of a bygone age provide many great photographic opportunities – as well as knot gardens full of herbs, old apple orchards, close-ups of seeds and fruit ripening in the sun – and don't forget the humble pot of tomatoes on the window sill! This category shows some great photos to whet the appetite.

People in the Garden

Gardens are for enjoyment – even if that enjoyment sometimes means hard work. Kids love to run around, while many of us will enjoy the round of the seasons – sowing, planting, clipping and harvesting. And then of course there's always that day when the garden is just for family and friends – good conversation or just plain relaxation. In this category, the judges looked for those pictures that really illustrate a passion for a personal retreat, a playground, or a workplace.

Plant Portraits

Achieving great images of plants and flowers requires skill, passion and commitment. This category celebrates the ephemeral beauty of the plant – from seed to compost. Plant portraiture is all about capturing the very essence, or character, of a plant. This could be a rambling rose or a humble bluebell, an exotic tree peony or the delicate flowerhead of a grass. A single bloom in isolation can be admired for its uniqueness.

Trees

This category celebrates the tree in all its diverse forms. From the gnarled old oak to the mighty redwood, photographers were invited to show us how important trees are in our lives and in the health of our planet. Winning images will reveal the treasures of our great world forests as well as the beauty of a solitary tree. How do people and trees live side by side in one world? How does a tree create a sense of well-being? Most of all, these photographs celebrate the simple beauty of our planet's trees.

Wildlife in the Garden

In a world where natural habitats are being depleted, gardens are a haven for wildlife. The wild creatures that use our gardens can become familiar companions, or rare and special visitors. These may be creatures that only you are privileged to see – a nocturnal hedgehog for example – or they could be tiny insects that are easily overlooked, except by the keen photographer. This category is about all the creatures that enjoy the garden, from beetles and butterflies to birds and badgers. These images display that moment where 'wildlife in the garden' becomes an inspiration.

Young International Garden Photographer of the Year

Under 16s were invited to enter single images into any of the above categories.

THE JUDGES

Chris Beardshaw
Award-winning garden designer

Award-winning garden designer Chris Beardshaw continues to flourish. With five RHS Gold Medals to his name and his ever increasing popularity, he has now received the 'People's Choice' Award at the Chelsea Flower Show for two years running. As an accomplished author, Chris has written two books, *The Natural Gardener* and *How Does Your Garden Grow?* and he is a regular columnist for the *Daily Mail* and *Period House* magazine. Central to much of his work is his desire to extend his knowledge to a wider audience with his lectures and talks around the country. Keen to promote horticulture to all, Chris strives to develop school projects and continues to devote time to a number of charities such as The Woodland Trust, The Wildlife Trust, WRAP, RSBP, RNLI, The Salvation Army, The National Lottery: Good Causes, and The Environment Agency. With the captivating and informative series of *The Great Garden Detectives* Chris's TV shows go from strength to strength.

Andrew Lawson
Garden photographer

Andrew Lawson is a well-known and highly respected garden photographer whose pictures have been reproduced extensively in books and magazines worldwide. Andrew is a keen gardener himself and his pictures are informed by a deep knowledge of the subject. He wrote and illustrated *The Gardener's Book of Colour* published by Frances Lincoln, and he has provided pictures for numerous books including those written by Rosemary Verey, Penelope Hobhouse, Roy Strong and HRH The Prince of Wales.

Clive Nichols
Garden photographer

Clive Nichols is one of the world's most successful flower and garden photographers. He has won many awards for his work and in 2005 was voted Garden Photographer of the Year by the Garden Writers Guild. His work has appeared in countless magazines, books and calendars throughout the world. He is in constant demand as a lecturer and teacher, running workshops for many clients, including the Royal Botanic Gardens, Kew and the Royal Horticultural Society. He has appeared on British and Japanese TV and sits on the RHS Photographic Committee. His most recent book is *The Art of Flower and Garden Photography*, which was published in association with the Royal Horticultural Society, by Argentum.

Laura Giuffrida
Exhibitions and Galleries Leader, Royal Botanic Gardens, Kew

With a background in art and design, including photography, Laura has spent much of her career working at Kew Gardens, where her main responsibility has been the management of Kew's exhibition programme. Examples include the development of the *Plants+People* exhibition, and the Orange Room at the Millennium Seed Bank, Wakehurst Place. She is also responsible for delivering temporary exhibitions at both sites, including *Gardens of Glass – Chihuly at Kew*, the co-curation of *Moore at Kew* and currently the development of exhibitions in the new Shirley Sherwood Gallery of Botanical Art at Kew.

THE JUDGES

Eddie Ephraums

Publishing consultant and commissioning editor of photography books

Through his publishing consultancy Envisage Books (www.envisagebooks.com), Eddie works with individual photographers and organisations to further develop their creative ideas and help ensure their art speaks to its intended audience. As part of that work, he also curates exhibitions (including the IGPOTY summer exhibition at Kew), plus he runs photography and book publishing workshops. He is the consultant editor of photography for Argentum books, responsible for commissioning a number of acclaimed titles, such as Joe Cornish's *First Light*. Eddie also produces his own photography books; currently he is working on a planned series called *A Photographer at Work*, the first being with Joe.

Victoria Skeet

Picture Library Manager, National Trust

Victoria Skeet has 20 years' experience in researching and editing images for commercial photo libraries, national newspapers, books and magazines. For the past nine years she has been working for The National Trust, commissioning and editing images of some of the world's most beautiful gardens and plant collections. Her knowledge and love of gardens is not limited to the grand and formal, as a dedicated allotment-holder she is just as passionate about the small, the humble and the much-loved plot of land.

Suzanne Sharrock

Director of Global Programmes, BGCI

Suzanne Sharrock is the Director of Global Programmes for Botanic Gardens Conservation International (BGCI), a membership organisation that brings together around 600 botanic gardens. Suzanne has been with BGCI for six years and is responsible for BGCI's communications, as well as leading scientific programmes that address the impacts of climate change on plant diversity. Suzanne is editor of BGCI's twice-yearly botanic garden journal (*BGjournal*) and oversees the production of all BGCI's technical publications. Suzanne also works on policy issues connected with the Global Strategy for Plant Conservation and provides support to the European Botanic Gardens Consortium. Before joining BGCI, Suzanne worked on plant conservation projects in Nepal, Australia, Papua New Guinea and the Caribbean.

Kathryn Bradley-Hole

Gardens Editor, Country Life *magazine*

As the gardens editor of *Country Life*, one of the UK's oldest weekly journals, Kathryn commissions plant and garden photography through every season for the magazine's discerning readership. Her latest books – *Lost Gardens of England* and *Villa Gardens of the Mediterranean* – are illustrated by atmospheric photographs she has drawn from *Country Life*'s 112-year-old picture archive, featuring work of some of the best garden photographers from generations past and present.

Heather Angel
Wildlife Photographer

Tony Kirkham
Head of Arboretum and Horticultural Services at the Royal Botanic Gardens, Kew

Damien Demolder
Editor, Amateur Photographer

David Watchus
Publisher, AA Media

Heather Angel began photographing when she used a camera to document marine life; this led to a career change and her images appearing worldwide.

As a wildlife photographer Heather has been at the forefront of wildlife photography in Britain for more than a quarter of a century. She has tutored the popular annual plant photography course at Kew since 1990. Heather manages her own image library (www.naturalvisions.co.uk) and has written 55 books. She is currently working on *Wild Kew*. She has received many awards including an honorary DSc from Bath University and a professorship from Nottingham University. Heather was President of the Royal Photographic Society from 1984-86.

With his roots firmly in the world of trees, Tony is Head of Arboretum and Horticultural Services at the Royal Botanic Gardens, Kew, where he looks after an amazing 14,000 specimens. Author and editor of countless publications on the subject of trees, Tony is also presenter of the two acclaimed BBC series, *The Trees that Made Britain*. With this wealth of experience, he is ideally placed to be our Guest Judge for the Trees category.

Damien Demolder has worked for *Amateur Photographer* (www.amateurphotographer. co.uk) for over ten years, moving from writing interviews and pieces on technique to camera and equipment reviews, until he become editor in 2006. An obsessive photographer as well as a journalist, his interests span every major photographic subject, for which he uses a wide range of ancient and modern film and digital cameras. Damien has his own personal galleries at www.damiendemolder.com

David Watchus took over as Publisher at the AA at the beginning of 2006, having worked in a variety of roles within the business. His vision is to build on AA Media's strong base in travel, lifestyle and map and atlas publishing, areas in which the AA has many market-leading titles, while increasing the presence of AA Media in the wider illustrated reference market.

David's involvement in International Garden Photographer of the Year is core to this vision and is also indicative of the quality of both production ideals and editorial integrity that is the cornerstone of the book-publishing ethos within AA Media.

ABOUT INTERNATIONAL GARDEN PHOTOGRAPHER OF THE YEAR

The first Garden Photographer of the Year exhibition, May 2008

1–The exhibition at the Royal Botanic Gardens, Kew.

2–Director of Kew Gardens, Professor Stephen Hopper, with the first Garden Photographer of the Year, Claire Takacs, alongside her winning image.

3–Fergus Gill, winner of the Young Garden Photographer of the Year award.

4–Henrique Souto, winner of the Portfolio category, accepts his award from Michele Channer of Calumet.

5–Colin Roberts alongside his winning image.

Photography by Emma Peios

Gardens are where nature and humanity meet in harmony. The outcomes of that meeting can be glorious not only for the gardener but for every person who sees that garden. This competition and exhibition is a place where that harmonious meeting is celebrated. Furthermore, it invites anyone with a camera to participate in that celebration.

Our hope is that everyone who enters the competition – whether they win a prize or not – will feel that their own appreciation of the garden and the plants around us has been heightened as a result of making their picture choices for the competition – trying a new technique – or perhaps looking at plants in a different way.

We hope that those who enter will learn and be inspired by the photographs they see in this book and at the exhibition. We, as organisers, are ourselves inspired by the people we meet and speak to both at the exhibition and in the course of the competition year.

The garden scenes depicted on these pages offer a pause for thought, a quietening of the breath, an opening of the eyes. Gardens are a haven not only for plants, not only for wildlife, but for us.

Philip Smith

To find out more about the competition visit www.igpoty.com

"The best thing for me has been all the people I have met as a result of the competition, and the huge amount of feedback I've received. I had an email from a woman who said just seeing the picture had made her happy. I would definitely encourage others to enter."

Claire Takacs
International Garden Photographer of the Year 2008

"I won the portfolio prize last year and want to tell of the enormous impact of the prize in my photographic life. I think that everyone who likes floral and garden photography must try this contest. All of us have something to learn from each other."

Henrique Souto
category winner, Best Portfolio 2008

"It has been pleasing to see the photograph published widely and the challenge for me as a photographer is to try and produce new images which have the same novelty and impact. In particular, the opportunity to capture common garden species in a new and interesting way is a great motivating factor and the competition provides me with an additional way of sharing some of my images with fellow wildlife enthusiasts."

Andrew Bailey
category winner, Wildlife in the Garden 2008

"The good fortune of winning the 'Trees' category in 2008 meant a great deal to me. I'm still amazed that something as simple as a native ash tree on a misty morning could bring me such good fortune. And meeting the other contestants at Kew Gardens was really special.

What's more, since winning the award I've had many contacts from like-minded people who have seen my image at the recent exhibitions. Without doubt my interest in trees and my passion for photography have been enhanced following my success in the competition."

Colin Roberts
category winner, Trees 2008

INTERNATIONAL
GARDEN
PHOTOGRAPHER OF THE YEAR

GARDEN VIEWS

JUDGE'S CHOICE

KURT TONG (p.34)

BIRDCAGES

This is a poignant image as the caged birds look onto

a painted mural of bamboo and wild birds. And yet the

cheerful colours of the cages bring a sense of joy. It makes

for a troubling and beautiful photograph and those conflicts

are what make this photograph so inspiring.

Victoria Skeet

INTERNATIONAL GARDEN PHOTOGRAPHER OF THE YEAR

OVERALL WINNER

JONATHAN BERMAN --->   FIRST

In Tresco Abbey Garden.
Tresco, Isles of Scilly, England.

This is an early-afternoon infrared view over Tresco Abbey Garden, looking south, with my daughter viewing the scene. A tiny, four-day-old crescent moon is just visible. I first visited Tresco and its gardens as a child, and I remembered it as a magical place. I did not return for many years until I came for holidays with my own children. I wanted to capture in this photograph my undiminished wonder at this special place. I used infrared – with its ability to darken skies and lighten foliage – to create the fairytale atmosphere. The inclusion of my daughter added depth. I had photographed this scene on several occasions but on this occasion the cloud patterns and presence of the moon lifted it out of the ordinary.

SAM STYLES SECOND

The Privy Garden in snow.
Hampton Court Palace, Surrey, England.

Living close by and working at Hampton Court has given me the chance to rush in when a photographic opportunity presents itself. This time it was waking up to snow, which I managed to photograph before anyone walked on it. The formal 18th-century Privy Garden, with its topiaried fastigiate yews (*Taxus baccata* 'Fastigiata') and mophead hollies emerging from clipped box parterres (*Buxus sempervirens*), is transformed by a blanket of snow and makes a fine sight.

CLAIRE TAKACS

Spring at King John's Lodge.
Etchingham, East Sussex, England.

I was visiting England from Australia, and hoping to find a few gardens to photograph. I spent some time at King John's Lodge and was immediately inspired by its beauty, which is particularly apparent in the early morning, when the light picks up and draws together the many different layers of the garden.

🌱 **CLAIRE TAKACS**   COMMENDED

Goegap Nature Reserve.
Northern Cape, South Africa.

I was visiting South Africa to photograph the spring wild flowers. Inspired by how different the landscape and plants were there, I wanted to show the garden, particularly the Quiver tree, in its unique setting, with the desert and mountains behind.

SUE STUBBS

Gardens are for pleasure.
M Central, Sydney, New South Wales, Australia.

The rooftop garden at M Central is an urban oasis of grasses and small, secluded havens, with a stunning view. The building has been converted into apartments from a wool store, but much of the original building and its character has been retained. Its dramatic architectural elements contrast with the flowing softness of the grasses, and those who live in the apartments fully appreciate and love the garden. The building fronts a main road but, once you are in the garden, the busy city seems far away. It is a little slice of heaven.

INTERNATIONAL GARDEN PHOTOGRAPHER OF THE YEAR

WINNING PORTFOLIO

Calumet Photographic is delighted to sponsor the Portfolio section of the second International Garden Photographer of the Year book.

The company first sowed the seeds of its retailing success in Chicago back in 1939 – now its branches flourish across the United States and Europe.
And in the UK the company has grown to become the leading professional photographic retailer; *it's where the pros go*.

Calumet's customers can purchase products and services, including a rapidly expanding Calumet 'own brand' range, over the counter at any of its stores, or they can purchase online.

Photographers looking to expand their knowledge can sign up to programme of seminars, which take place in purpose-built seminar rooms at key branches and cover a wide range of photography disciplines.

Find us online at www.calumetphotographic.co.uk and sign up for our regular e-newsletters and widely acclaimed *Focus* magazine packed with latest product news, features and 'photographers at work' case studies.

JUDGE'S CHOICE

SEBASTIAN KAPS (pp.30–31)

GEORGENGARTEN

Sebastian Kaps has captured the unique atmosphere of this stunning landscape garden in the depths of a bitterly cold German winter. The brilliant winter light, combined with the dark, brooding skies create a cinematic drama to each scene. Each picture is beautifully composed and the result is a dramatic and striking portfolio.

Clive Nichols

SEBASTIAN KAPS   WINNER

Georgengarten, Dessau, Germany.

The Georgengarten is one of the biggest parks in the Dessau-Wörlitz Garden Realm, a UNESCO World Heritage site. Prince Johann Georg von Anhalt (1748-1811), brother of Prince Franz, built the palace and its surroundings with the help of the architects JF Eyserbeck and JG Schoch – to complement the Wörlitz Park. A 50-acre garden surrounds the Georgium Castle and stretches as far as the River Elbe. Within the park many classical buildings, smaller examples of architecture and sculptures can be found working in harmony with their surroundings.

3

4

5

6

Fuji FinePix S3 Pro, 10mm to 70mm zoom lens settings

1–*The Seven Columns* The 7 Columns in morning fog (-15°C).
2–*Monopterus* The Ionic Temple (or Monopterus) at Georgengarten.
3–*The Bevernvase* The Bevernvase at Beckerbruch (a part of the Georgengarten).
4–*Georgium Palace in the evening* Georgium Palace was built in 1782 in the classical style by Friedrich Wilhelm von Erdmannsdorff. The palace is surrounded by Georgengarten park with numerous early classical-style buildings. Georgium Palace is a UNESCO World Heritage site.
5–*Two Willows* Snow-covered willows at the entrance to the so-called Viereckteich.
6–*The Ruined Bridge* The so-called Ruined Bridge at the Beckerbruch (part of the Georgengarten).

NICOLA STOCKEN TOMKINS COMMENDED

Winter dawn.
Pembury House, Clayton, East Sussex, England.

This is a small woodland of birch, alder, beech, chestnut, witch hazel and field maple that form a leafy canopy in summer, but are stripped in winter to reveal carpets of snowdrops, hellebores and aconites beneath. As the sun rises higher, it forces itself through the naked trees, forming pools of light that illuminate clump after clump of flowers that carpet the woodland floor.

NICHOLAS HASTINGS-WINCH COMMENDED

The circle.
Eaton Hall, Cheshire, England.

I photographed this circle of clipped yew trees (*Taxus baccata*) at dawn on a frosty December morning. It was taken looking towards the enclosed rose gardens, with the sun rising above the scattered cloud on the horizon. The frost on the grass gave the lawn a pastel green quality, which contrasted with the very dark green of the yews. As the sun rose above the horizon a faint mist added to the atmosphere.

KURT TONG

FINALIST

SOULA ZAVACOPOULOS

COMMENDED

Birdcages.
Guangzhou Zoo, Guangzhou, Guangdong Sheng, China.

The image is taken from the series 'People's Park', which documents the current state of public parks in China, once important cultural and societal spaces that have gone through great changes as China progresses. It was taken in the 'Chinese Garden' section within Guangzhou Zoo, which also houses the avian species.

Outside in.
London, England.

The car pictured was parked in a residential street in bustling central London. The owner of the car has created their own 'garden' in a cramped, busy city – their own personal version of a natural retreat, including grass, flowers, birds and a dog. The photo explores our relationship with gardens and challenges our perception of what a garden actually is, what they mean to us in our modern-day lives and what relationship we have with them. Not everyone has the outdoor space for a garden. However, the need to interact with and create them (whatever their form) is clearly still inherently strong.

⁂ SIMON GRIFFITHS ⋯⋯⋗   FINALIST

The Leeming garden.
Mornington Peninsula, Victoria, Australia.

The Leeming garden uses a lot of native planting materials indigenous to Victoria's
Mornington Peninsula. This was a commissioned photograph for *Belle* magazine.

COMMENDED

Cruden Farm.
Langwarrin, Victoria, Australia.

The driveway at Cruden Farm is planted with lemon-scented gums (*Eucalyptus citriodora*).
This was a commissioned photograph for a book called *Period Gardens* by Myles Baldwin.

CAROLE DRAKE   COMMENDED

Welford Park.
Newbury, Berkshire, England.
Courtesy of Mrs J Puxley.

Mist rises from the River Lambourn as it gently flows through a landscape encrusted with snowdrops and aconites below soaring limes laden with mistletoe. At the centre lies an exquisitely symmetrical Queen Anne house and a formal rose garden, which is monochromatic and mysterious at this time of year. The combination of water, snowdrops and the presence of massive, sculptural trees is intensely thrilling.

Nikon D200

I was inspired by the snowdrop display of course, but also the way in which the wider landscape and the garden simply bleed into each other, everything watery and fluid. I was very lucky that it was a perfect morning, clear and still.

MARY KOCOL

Lilac landscape.
The Arnold Arboretum, Boston, Massachusetts, USA.

The Arnold Arboretum has a gorgeous collection of lilacs, almost 400 plants in 200 varieties. Every May it celebrates Lilac Sunday at the peak of the season. The variety of lilacs and richness of purples caught my attention in this particular view of the Arboretum. I especially like the juicy purples in the foreground and how variations of the colour reach into the background. The picture was made the day after Lilac Sunday, after the crowds had gone. It was late in the afternoon, the sun was in and out, and the occasional breeze carried the fragrant lilac scent through the air. It was lovely to be there – a quintessential spring moment in New England. *Courtesy Gallery NAGA, Boston, Massachusetts.*

YOSHKO PALENIK

Morning walk.
The Royal Botanic Gardens, Kew, Surrey, England.

The silhouettes of two figures are captured walking through the gardens at Kew in the misty sunshine early one morning. The misty atmosphere, full of sunshine and beautiful autumnal colours, amazed me.

FINALIST

Japanese gardens in fall.
Portland Japanese Garden, Portland, Oregon, USA.

Various fall-coloured Japanese maple trees (*Acer palmatum*) came into peak fall colour at the same time. I had been to these gardens dozens of times over a period of 20 years, but had never been able to capture the trees at their absolute peak.

ROB WHITWORTH COMMENDED

Early summer in a Wiltshire garden.
Goulters Mill Farm, Wiltshire, England.

This inspirational garden was a wonderful assault on the senses during this beautiful early
June morning. Designed by Alison Harvey, strong verticals are provided by the cream-
apricot spires of *Eremurus* x *isebellinus* 'Cleopatra' and the prickly, silver Scottish thistle
Onopordium acanthium.

⚜ JASON LISKE   COMMENDED

MARTYN GREENHALGH ⤵   COMMENDED

Water garden.
Lagunitas, California, USA.

Garden ornament behind a screen of foliage.
William Kent garden, Rousham, Oxfordshire, England.

This magnificent native site inspired me one sunrise. Large-scale indigenous grasslands collide with natural pool elements in this very sculptural garden that celebrates the incredible borrowed views to the south and the west. Seasonal patterns such as wind, fog, and light quality transform the space through time. There is no irrigation for this garden and it utilises all native plantings.

It was a combination of the quality of light and the shape of the urn behind the screen of the foliage that appealed to me. This glimpse is, for me, typical of a certain type of classical English garden, particularly Rousham.

ANDREA JONES

COMMENDED

FINALIST

Lurie Gardens.
Millennium Park, Chicago, Illinois, USA.

The Lurie Gardens were designed by Gustafson Guthrie Nichol Ltd, Piet Oudolf and Robert Israel. They feature a large perennial meadow, which includes native American plants, including a white form of the coneflower (*Echincea purpurea*).
From the book *Great Gardens of America*, by Tim Richardson.

Thomas Jefferson's Monticello Gardens.
Charlottesville, Virginia, USA.

Thomas Jefferson was one of the founding fathers of North America. His garden is a botanic showpiece, a source of food, and an experimental laboratory of ornamental and useful plants from around the world.

WORLD BOTANIC GARDENS

The Role of Botanic Gardens

Botanic gardens have had a changing role throughout history, beginning as medicinal gardens for the study and cultivation of plants with healing properties and going through many phases including, of course, as pleasure gardens.

In current times, they are becoming key players in both the conservation of plants and in providing inspirational experiences for the people who come to see them. They also have a vital role to play in the mitigation of the effects of climate change. As custodians of both plant collections and specialist plant knowledge, botanic gardens are perfectly positioned to help people adapt to new climates in different regions through conserving carbon sinks and in the sustainable use of plants.

There are now many botanic gardens working in collaboration across the world. Botanic Gardens Conservation International is an international organisation, based at Kew Gardens, that represents over 600 members – mostly botanic gardens – in over 120 countries. BGCI, with partners like Kew, is working to ensure the worldwide conservation of threatened plants, the continued existence of which are intrinsically linked to global issues including poverty, human well-being and climate change.

Royal Botanic Gardens, Kew, and Botanic Garden Conservation International are proud to support International Garden Photographer of the Year

BGCI
Plants for the Planet

Botanic Garden Conservation International

BGCI was founded in 1987 to link botanic gardens as a co-operating global network for effective plant conservation. It now links over 2500 institutions in more than 120 countries, all working together to preserve and promote plant diversity for people and the planet.

Our vision is 'a world in which plant diversity is valued, secure and supporting all life' and to create this world our mission is 'to mobilise botanic gardens and engage partners in securing plant diversity for the well-being of people and the planet'.

JUDGE'S CHOICE

JUNE KINGSBURY (p.62)

THE EDEN PROJECT

This image for me captures many of the key elements of a botanic garden. The naturalistic planting of colourful, carnivorous plants in the foreground illustrates the beauty and diversity of plants in the wild, while the looming reflection of the biome highlights the growing need to protect the world's flora in the face of today's rapidly changing climate.

Suzanne Sharrock

🎋 MATTHEW BISHOP FIRST

The Alpine House.
The Royal Botanic Gardens, Kew, Surrey, England.

I wanted to create an image that depicts Kew in the 21st century. The recently opened Davies Alpine House not only provides a unique opportunity to view alpines outside of their native habitats, but is also an excellent example of contemporary design in a modern botanic garden. The evening light on the grass provided a fantastic frame for the ethereal glow emanating from the Alpine House. I found the angle I wanted for the shot but had to wait until the light was perfect to achieve the desired result.

ANDY SMALL ⋯⟫ SECOND

Castle Rock, Kirstenbosch.
Kirstenbosch National Botanical Garden, Cape Town, South Africa.

After spending a few days at Kirstenbosch, I knew, at this time of the year, that the sun would set directly behind Castle Rock. I wanted to capture the drama of this and the Strelitzia (*Strelitzia reginae*) provided colour and movement in the foreground.

🌱 NIKKI DE GRUCHY   THIRD

Simulation.
The Eden Project, Cornwall, England.

'Simulation' hints at the alternative interpretations of this image. The biome at the Eden Project enables the simulation of a tropical rainforest environment in the temperate English climate. In its hexagonal structure and maintenance walkway we see a resemblance to the simple elements of a flower head and stem, as might be drawn by a child.

JUNE KINGSBURY ···>   FINALIST

Leaf lily.
Water Lily House, The Royal Botanic Gardens, Kew, Surrey, England.

I found this leaf from the Santa Cruz water lily (*Victoria cruziana*) floating upside down and loved the reflection of the roof struts in the water. The Santa Cruz water lily was originally discovered in 1801 in Bolivia, and named after Queen Victoria. The reflections of the roof of the Water Lily House mimic the ribs of the leaf.

❀ DAMIAN GILLIE ⤳   COMMENDED

Bird of paradise flower (*Strelitzia reginae*).
Cambridge University Botanic Garden, Cambridge, England.

This bird of paradise flower was found in front of the new 'Continents Apart' glasshouse. Here we can see plants from southwest Australia and the cape of South Africa, which were once joined as the ancient landmass of Gondwanaland. Most of these plants are unique to these two areas of the world, and many are dependent on bush fires for regeneration. A world away from the freezing January conditions outside, this image illustrates the haven of warmth and colour on the inside. I come many times to this place in the winter months, and it feels different each time I visit. It is usually empty of people. This is just next to the entrance and so is the first and last thing I see as I arrive and leave.

Ficus species and a black-bold Philodendron leaf.
Tropical Glasshouse, Cambridge University Botanic Garden, Cambridge, England.

This rubber plant leaf was hanging in front of a Philodendron leaf in the Cambridge University Botanic Garden. The rubber plant leaf is about six inches long, the Philodendron leaf some eight times longer. The contrast of the delicate light green and the heavy blue-green fascinated me, situated at the heart of this amazing tropical glasshouse. The smells, the warmth, the extraordinary plants from the world's most exotic places contrast so completely with the freezing January conditions outside. Only the silence is constant and unexpected. I first photographed the Philodendron leaf through a cluster of other foliage, but then went back to create a simpler image with just two leaves. The rubber plant leaf is a few inches from the lens while the Philodendron is some three feet away against the wall.

DAVID MAITLAND FINALIST

Palm House bracket.
The Royal Botanic Gardens, Kew, Surrey, England.

The giant Palm House at Kew is a masterpiece of Victorian design. I love the spectacular design and attention to detail that fits this building so purposefully with its function of housing tropical plants. The elaborate brackets bracing the iron dome steel frame echo the tendrils of a vine, and I wanted to show this.

CAROLINE AMES FINALIST

Silent odyssey.
RHS Wisley, Surrey, England.

I took this photograph of the Glasshouse at Wisley on a bitterly cold day in January, just as the mist was just beginning to rise above the lake. I wanted to capture the timeless beauty of nature beside Wisley's stunning vision for the future. There was not a breath of wind and the utter stillness created perfect mirror-image reflections.

BAPI CHAKRABORTY   FINALIST

Conservation.
Bloedel Conservatory, Queen Elizabeth Park, Vancouver, Canada.

This is the Bloedel Conservatory in Queen Elizabeth Park, Vancouver, with a primarily tropical ecosystem. The warmed dome was in stark contrast to the chilly, un-tropical winter evening during which I took this picture; a futuristic bubble of lush green life. It was a personal haven during grey days. The condensation on the unique dome from the cooling dusk created mysterious visual effects and streak patterns.

DANNY BEATH ···⊱   COMMENDED

The Climatron.
Missouri Botanical Garden, St Louis, Missouri, USA.

At 140 feet high and 300 feet across, the iconic Climatron is the largest biodome on earth. The picture shows a reflection in the water lily pool, where the angel sculptures stand. I knew this scene would look good at sunset as a reflection, with the combination of the lights around the pool and the stark shapes making a dramatic silhouette.

JOHN QUINTERO COMMENDED

Palm House.
Royal Botanic Garden, Edinburgh, Scotland.

I visited the Royal Botanic Garden in February 2008. It was a terrible, rainy day and I almost went back to my hotel, but I decided to wait for a while. When the rain ceased, the light was amazing, and I took some photos of the Palm House with the beautiful clouds in the background. I included the branches of a tree in the foreground to frame the building. Because of the rain, the entire garden was almost empty, which made it easier to compose.

JEFF EDEN COMMENDED

Palm House at sunrise.
The Royal Botanic Gardens, Kew, Surrey, England.

I was commissioned to photograph the cover for the 250th anniversary souvenir issue of *Kew Magazine*. They wanted an image that celebrated Kew, and I wanted to photograph the Palm House in a way I hadn't seen before. I knew the type of shot I wanted to achieve and BBC weather finally indicated the perfect morning after a month of greyness. After a very early start I got the sunrise shot I was after.

JUNE KINGSBURY COMMENDED

STEVE REW COMMENDED

The Eden Project.
Bodelva, Cornwall, England.

The biome is immediately recognisable but in this photograph it is only partially visible as a reflection in the water. In the foreground are pitcher plants (or *Sarracenia*), which lure insects with nectar and use their elongated tube-shaped leaves filled with water and digestive enzymes to catch and consume them.

In front of the Palm House.
The Royal Botanic Gardens, Kew, Surrey, England.

The photograph was taken on a December afternoon, with low, raking light shining through the Palm House and fountain. I pointed my camera towards the sun, to capture the light in the water and the silhouette of the statue and Palm House.

THAMER AL-TASSAN

Nan Lian Garden Bridge.
Nan Lian Garden, Hong Kong.

I was inspired by the golden orange colour of the bridge against the background greenery.

🌴 **ANDREA JONES**   Finalist

Bridge to Evening Island.
Chicago Botanic Garden, Illinois, USA.

The curvy footbridge at Chicago Botanic Garden leads to Evening Island, where landscape
architects from Oehme van Sweden have planted a stunning combination of perennial
grasses, trees and shrubs.

THE EDIBLE
GARDEN

JUDGE'S CHOICE

DEE FISH (p.69)

FRESHLY PICKED
SWEET BASIL LEAVES

I loved the simplicity of this image. The contrast between the cold, hard surface of the pot and the vibrant, lively green of the basil leaves is perfectly balanced.

David Watchus

BAPI CHAKRABORTY First

Tomatoes with attitude.
Vancouver, Canada.

These tomatoes not only had attitude, but also possessed powerful sculptural qualities. I never realised tomatoes could be this sexy...

DEE FISH Second

Freshly picked sweet basil leaves (*Basilicum*).
Basildon, Essex, England.

I love the smell of basil, and wanted somehow to evoke this in my image, so emphasised the deep, saturated green of the leaves.

JO WHITWORTH

THIRD

Prize-winning onion 'Kelsae'.
The Royal Horticultural Halls, London, England.

This prize-winning onion, entered by Mr H Thomas, was on display at the Royal Horticultural Society's annual autumn show, and just cried out for a close-up. 'Biggest vegetable' competitions still hold great appeal all over the country, and this is what attracted me to document the event.

RICHARD FREESTONE

COMMENDED

Half-used garlic bulb.

I had been watching this garlic bulb as its cloves gradually disappeared into various recipes, so aimed to capture its simple, graphic beauty.

 **JOHANNA PARKIN**

Wine bouquet.
London, England.

I made the shape of a wine glass out of rosemary, dill, chervil, white and purple lavender and strawberries – the bouquet of flavours found in certain white wines.

JO HOLDING ···>

Mr McGregor's garden.
Beningbrough Hall, York, North Yorkshire, England.
By kind permission of the National Trust;
www.nationaltrust.org

The walled kitchen garden at Beningbrough Hall is now in the care of the National Trust. This is the glass house, with red oak leaf and butter lettuce in the foreground, and espalier pear, apple and fig trees against the Georgian brick wall. There are various herbs in pots, grape vines and traditional wooden cloches protecting tender lettuce shoots. I found the dense profusion of fruit and vegetables very inspiring. The neat box hedging and wooden cloches were quintessentially English, like a perfect scene from Beatrix Potter's *The Tale of Peter Rabbit*.

JONATHAN BUCKLEY ····⟩   FINALIST

Sarah Raven holding a container of harvested forced chicory 'Witloof' and 'Rossa di Treviso'.
Audley End House and Gardens, Essex, England.

I was working with Sarah Raven on an article about the chicory forcing sheds at Audley End. It was important to convey the fact that it was winter. I had taken a few still life shots of the chicory in a wooden box, but they lacked vitality. Having Sarah hold the colander made the shot much more interesting. It was a very cold day and it was lucky that Sarah was wearing this particular coat, scarf and gloves. The lighter chicory stood out brightly against the dark coat and the colours of gloves and scarf complemented the red chicory well.

Stripping redcurrants with a fork.
Sarah Raven's garden, Perch Hill, East Sussex,
England.

I was working with Sarah Raven on a cookery and gardening book, and I felt it was important to inject as much colour and action as possible into the garden and food images. Still images can be quite static so it makes a change to try and capture a sense of movement.

SUE STUBBS

The Edible Garden

With this portfolio I wanted to convey the sheer beauty of both everyday and exotic edibles. Their shape, colour and texture is shown in its simplest and purest form, each against a background painted with acrylics, while the colour and texture gives a different complexion to these fruit and vegetables, which are often taken for granted.

Canon EOS-1D Mk III, Canon EF 24-70mm f/2.8 lens.
The idea was to use these simple shapes in natural light to create a still life study with softness and depth that would draw you into the image. The backgrounds were layered with paint to add rich colour and texture, creating a painterly mood.

1

2

3

4

1–*Pumpkin* Golden nugget pumpkin on orange background.
2–*Beetroot* Beetroot on red background.
3–*Zucchini* Round grey zucchini on grey background.
4–*Plum* Plum on red background.
5–*Pomegranate* Pomegranate on red background.
6–*Apple* Delicious apple on grey background.

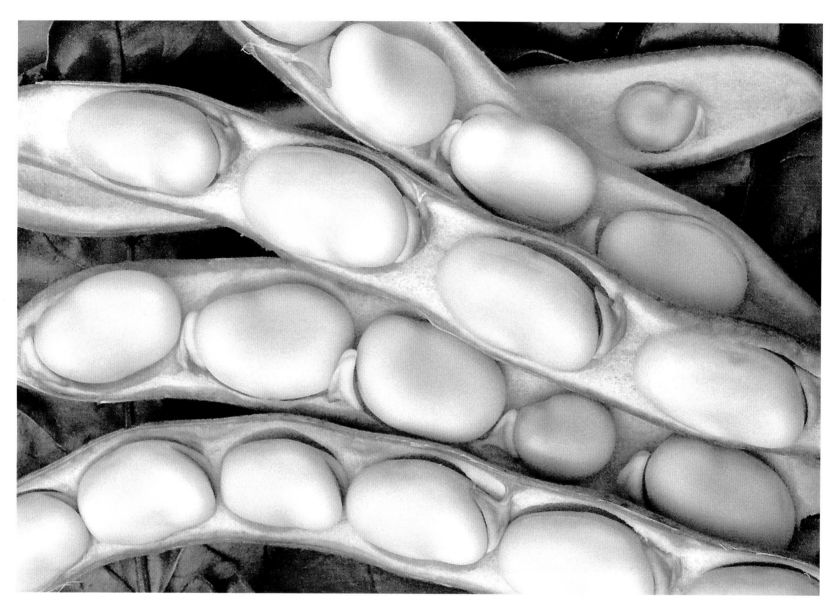

🌱 **WILLIAM BROAD**   COMMENDED

Broad beans.
Aunt Doll's garden, Wheatlow Brook, Staffordshire, England.

While my wife picked and prepared some broad beans for dinner, I noticed the contrast in texture between the freshly picked beans and the fur inside their pods.

Aubergines 'Farmer's Long' with borlotto bean 'Firetongue'.

The strips of vibrant colour, broken up by the speckled bean, create an almost abstract image.

PAUL DEBOIS   FINALIST

Pumpkins and squashes.
Styling by Abigail Dodd.

The brief for this studio photograph, taken for BBC *Gardeners' World* magazine, was quite simple – to give a warm, autumnal feel for a feature about pumpkins. I wanted to create a traditional atmosphere, so a hessian cloth background was the obvious starting point. As time was short, the lighting had to be simple, and one light with a reflector was perfect for a classic still life.

JOE FAIRS ···⟩   COMMENDED

Fallen apples.
Gestingthorpe, Essex, England.

I had returned home from a photographic outing, frustrated by my attempts to capture an image that summed up the autumn season, when I noticed these apples lying on the ground in my own garden. There was something about them that gave the impression of lost souls at sea.

ANDY PHILLIPSON ⋯⟩   COMMENDED

Enoki mushrooms.
National Farmers' Union stand, RHS Chelsea Flower Show, London, England.

Enoki are popular in Asian cuisine and are found in dishes ranging from soups to salads. This cultivated variety (which is grown in darkness) differs considerably from the more classically shaped wild Enokitake mushroom. The shape of the cultivated form is achieved by restricting the mushroom's growth using shaped cones. With this study I wanted to explore the otherworldly nature of these diminutive fungi and to capture the abstract nature of their interplay. I am fascinated by micro-landscapes, with their minute scale, and so also wanted to portray the mushrooms as being almost forest-like.

···▶ DAVID MAITLAND   FINALIST

Velvet shank fungus (*Flammulina velutipes*).
Calne, Wiltshire, England.

This edible fungus grows on deciduous trees – a young dead oak,
in this case. I love fungi. Not only are many of them good to eat, but
also they have a wonderful and beautiful architecture.

GARY ROGERS FINALIST

JOHANNA PARKIN ⋯⋅ COMMENDED

The gourd tunnel.
Château de Valmer, Vouvray, France.

Runner beans.
London, England.

The pergola that contains the Lagenaria National Collection of gourds is a full 110 metres long, and features almost every size and form of these fascinating plants. It was just one highlight in an assignment to photograph the castle gardens of the Loire.

I love the bold, natural, healthy green of runner beans, and the graphic yet imperfectly wobbly lines their sides form when clustered together. This gives them character as a group of vegetables. I photographed this group of scarlet runner beans, grown organically in my friend's vegetable garden, from overhead and against a black background, so the edges would gleam out of the darkness.

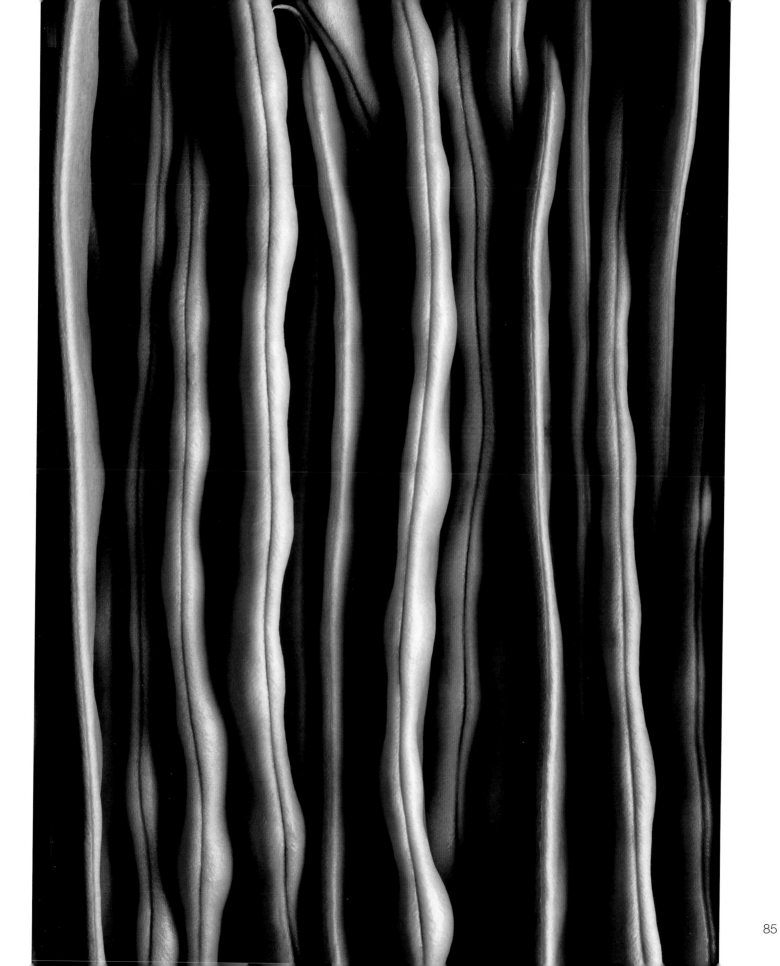

PEOPLE IN THE
GARDEN

JUDGE'S CHOICE

MAGGIE LAMBERT (p.90)

RUSTIC RETREAT

As this picture passed up and up through the judging stages,

we started referring to it as 'Solzhenitsyn'. The man reading in his

summerhouse has a physical resemblance to the great Russian

author – and to Tolstoy too. The picture has stillness and repose,

symmetry and balance that I admire immensely. It's too good to

have been posed. It's a 'seen' image. Maggie says it all in her own

description. I agree that each of the eight windows is a picture in

itself. Through the windows we see inside the old summerhouse

and, by reflection, the garden too. And in observing the man,

we also see his own implied 'reflection' – in the book that he is

reading with such concentration.

Andrew Lawson

43 gardeners' hands.

'43 gardeners' hands' is a series of portraits of some of the UK's best-known gardeners, as seen through their hands. Inspired by the fantastic working collages produced by the botanical photographer Karl Blossfeldt in the late 1920s, whose work was almost anatomical, I wanted to produce a montage that turned each pair of hands into a botanical specimen, reversing the effect of his work. This montage contains the hands of 43 gardeners, ranging from Alan Titchmarsh and the current *Gardeners' World* team and *Gardeners' Question Time* presenters, to award-winning designers, nurserymen, experts and journalists. Each person has a passion in his or her field, and also a character which can be seen through their most versatile tool.

I Bunny Guinness II Nigel Colborn III Bob Flowerdew IV & V Emma Townshend VI Joe Swift
VII Adam Pasco VIII & IX Cleve West X Rosie Atkins XI Stephen Lacey XII James Alexander-Sinclair
XIII John Cushnie XIV Arabella Lennox-Boyd XV & XVI Alan Titchmarsh XVII & XVIII Beth Chatto
XIX & XX Rachel de Thame XXI Matthew Wilson XXII Matthew Biggs XXIII Barbara Collecott
XXIV Jim Gardiner XXV Jim Arbury XXVI Guy Barter XXVII Andrew Lawson XXVIII Dan Pearson
XXIX Juliet Roberts XXX Mary Keen XXXI Tania Compton XXXII Pippa Greenwood
XXXIII Professor Stephen Hopper XXXIV Nigel Taylor XXXV Tony Kirkham XXXVI Chris Beardshaw
XXXVII Jekka McVicar XXXVIII Carol Klein XXXIX Roy Lancaster XL Alys Fowler
XLI Toby Buckland XLII Fergus Garrett XLIII Andy Sturgeon XLIV John Brookes
XLV Marina Christopher XLVI Judy Medhurst XLVII Peter Catt XLVIII & XLIX Ann-Marie Powell.

🌱 **MAGGIE LAMBERT**   SECOND

Rustic retreat.

The old summerhouse, which is situated in the shade of trees at the bottom of our garden, is a peaceful and private place (when no photographers are around) where a person can sit, read and enjoy the surroundings. The little building is now well integrated into the mature garden and birds and other wildlife felt comfortable coming near. I noticed that the reflections blended inside with outside, dissolving the walls of the building and enclosing the reader in a dreamlike world. Also I found the division into eight miniature images interesting – each surprisingly different.

🎗 **KEVIN COZMA**   THIRD

Promenade.
Ritsurin Park, Takamatsu, Kagawa, Japan.

This photograph was taken during an evening illumination at Ritsurin Park. Thousands
of people come here every spring to have picnics with friends and family under the
canopy of cherry blossom. An off-camera flash, tripod, and star-cross filter were used to
help make this picture.

ANNIE WILLIAMS FINALIST

Elsie in her garden.
Dwygyfylchi, Penmaenmawr, Conwy, North Wales.

This is a photograph of my friend Elsie in her beautiful garden. Aged 88, Elsie does all the work in the garden herself, including mowing the lawns. It is an extensive garden in a classic cottage style that displays her intuitive and creative sense of colour and design. Cultivated plants sit alongside wild flowers, giving a vibrant and unique quality to the garden. I wanted to celebrate Elsie's achievements as an amateur gardener who has exceptional creative skills and has spent her life creating this beautiful environment. I also wanted to express my admiration for her keeping so fit, healthy and independent.

KEVIN COZMA FINALIST

Nature girl.
Ritsurin Park, Takamatsu, Kagawa, Japan.

This is a picture of my beautiful daughter perched on my not so beautiful feet under a tree in Ritsurin Park, Japan. This is one of the most famous parks in Japan, and is a must-see for anyone who ventures to the island of Shikoku. I shot this with a wideangle lens while lying on a bench under the tree.

LIZ EDDISON COMMENDED

Jim Keeling at work.
Whichford Pottery, Shipston-on-Stour, Warwickshire, England.

Whichford Pottery, founded by Jim Keeling in 1976, is a family-run business making hand-thrown terracotta pots. This photograph of Jim was taken in his private studio at the pottery, while he worked on a commission to create a replica of an early watering can for the Garden Museum. I frequently photograph the magnificent hand-thrown pots at Whichford Pottery, but this was the first time I'd shown the potters at work.

ADRIENNE BROWN ···> FINALIST

Gardening boss.

This photograph shows my mother directing the proceedings as we cleared the garden following my daughter's wedding reception, making good for winter. My mother has a lifetime's interest in, and knowledge of gardening and, although suffering from dementia, has retained the ability to pass on all her tips and wisdom to the rest of the family. The flowers in the background are Cosmos and sweet peas, which I grew from seeds especially for the wedding. I planted them in beds and containers and they flowered brilliantly all summer, making a great backdrop for the celebrations. Seeing my mother sitting peacefully and thoroughly at home in the garden inspired me to try to capture that particular moment which, to me, seemed both sad and happy.

DAVID THURSTON

FINALIST

Nasturtiums.
Lhasa, Tibet.

Lhasa is 3,650 metres above sea level. The air is thin, winters are long, and vegetation is sparse. The colours of nature are few, so it was unusual to see this bank of nasturtiums in full bloom. Also growing, apparently in old tin cans, are some dahlias and geraniums. While walking, I stopped to photograph this splash of clear colour. I was moved by the idea that the very same flowers grow in my garden in Devon. A door creaked open, the curtain was pulled back and out came two lads in monks' robes to see what I was doing. What a bonus.

DAVID THURSTON　　　　　　　　　　　　　　　　FINALIST

Gates of Eden.
Viñales, Cuba.

Along a street in the small town of Viñales, Cuba, is a gate into a leafy front garden which, in another owner's hands, would perhaps shelter a car. Of course, I had to make a photograph of this gate and its bizarre slices of the citrus family. Some kind of vegetarian voodoo? Out popped the woman. For a happy dollar, she showed off the tropical wonderland she and her elder sister had created out back. The fruit? No idea. The great thing about allowing the camera to lead the way is the people you meet as you go. The chance encounter and the decisive moment rate as top thrills when you let the camera do the asking.

✝ **SONIA QUINLAN**   COMMENDED

On my own.
Linden, Michigan, USA.

The first major snowfall of the year brought Lex out to the garden path. With his trusty turtle on his back, he set out to explore the new world brought by winter. Lex was three years old at the time, and able to walk in the deep snow for the first time. He insisted on wearing his backpack, and I love what it adds to the image. I wanted to juxtapose my son with the vast horizon beyond the barn to illustrate how large the world must be in the eyes of such a little guy.

ANNE GILBERT ---} COMMENDED

Running from the rain.
Packwood House, Lapworth, Warwickshire, England.
By kind permission of the National Trust.
www.nationaltrust.org

This pathway runs along the top of the walled garden at Packwood House. There are mixed flower borders along each side, planted in hot colours. While taking shelter from a heavy downpour there, I thought I'd try to capture the beauty of the gardens in the rain. Just as I pressed the shutter to capture the scene, George ran into frame – the result of which is a lovely action shot. George's mother was sheltering next to me and gave me permission to enter the photo in this competition.

⊹···· SARAH WENBAN   COMMENDED

Rumi.
Sussex, England.

The briefest of moments – a fleeting kiss between a mother and
her little son – captured on a glorious summer day in their own
garden. The main feature of my portrait work combines my passion
for working outdoors using natural light, with natural environments
which have some emotional attachment for the subject – often their
own gardens. In this case, the family was emigrating to New Zealand
and they were sad to be leaving behind their beautiful English
garden. I wanted to give them pictures to remember the garden
and its atmosphere.

↑ JULIETTE WILES   COMMENDED

A break from the classroom.
Kyoto Botanical Garden, Kyoto, Japan.

The image shows a group of young Japanese school children in Kyoto Botanical Garden, gazing in awe at a row of Echium 'Pink Fountain'. The children were very excited; darting from one flowerbed to the next. When they saw these mysterious, tall plants, they rushed over and actually stopped and stood still for a couple of seconds, momentarily mesmerised by their unusual shape and size.

GERALD MAJUMDAR ⋯⟩   COMMENDED

Tim.
Comely Bank, Kidderminster, Worcestershire, England.

Retired GP Dr Tim Wadsworth, who is a friend of mine, was working in his garden and I wanted to show the enjoyment that he derives from hard work and the beautiful garden he has created.

PLANT
PORTRAITS

JUDGE'S CHOICE

NIGEL BURKITT (p.113)

MOUNT COOK LILY

To find a flowering wild specimen in pristine condition, under glorious weather and aligned with a backdrop which emphatically illustrates its habitat is the goal of those of us who enjoy plants in their wild habitats. The photographer of the Mount Cook lily tells us much about this endearing alpine plant in a fine and very beautiful shot.

Kathryn Bradley-Hole

DAVID MAITLAND (pp.120–121)

PLANTSCAPES

This is an exceptional collection of images – each is a wonder on its own, but together they form a thrilling experience. The subjects are terrifyingly delicate, but it's obvious they have been arranged with considerable love and care to create these gorgeous compositions.

Damien Demolder

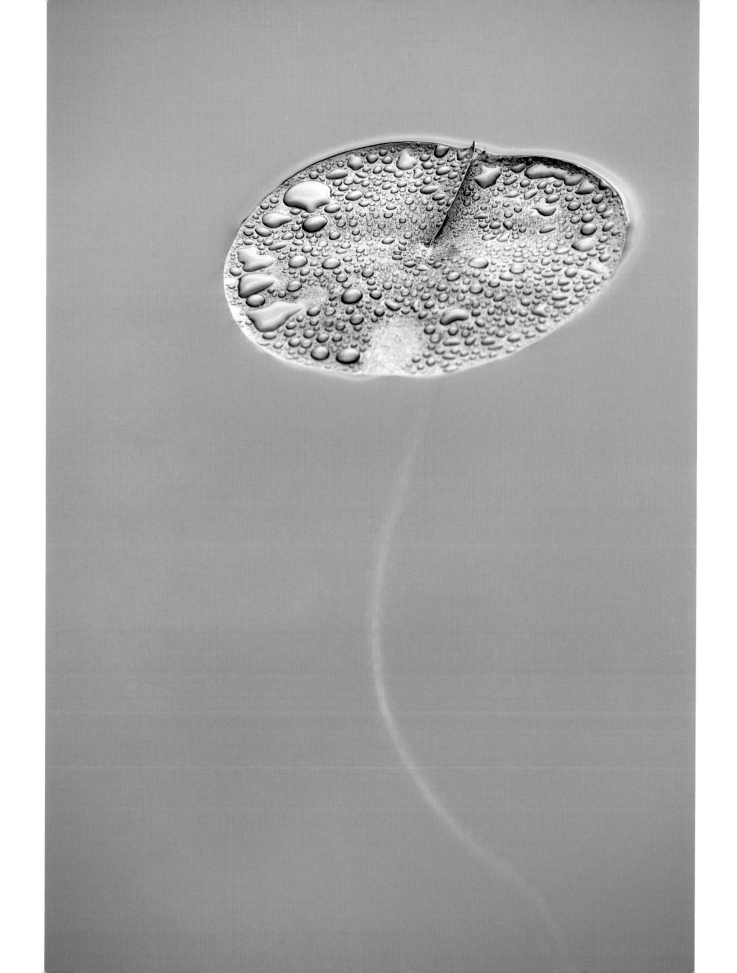

DEBORAH CASSO

First

Lone lily pad.
Washington Park Arboretum, Seattle, Washington State, USA.

A single lily pad with iridescent tones floats gracefully on the water of Union Bay in the Washington Park Arboretum. The simplicity of the subject, the interesting colours, and the grace of the lines in the image all inspired me to take this photograph.

KARIN GOLDBACH

Second

Romantic plants.
Lemgo, Germany.

This purple and white snake's head fritillary (*Fritillaria meleagris*) bloomed in my garden last spring. I took this photograph as the flower's delicate petals glowed in the sunlight. Gardening is my hobby and I spend a lot of time in mine. This allows me to observe and try to capture the countless variations of light, shadow, colour and mood.

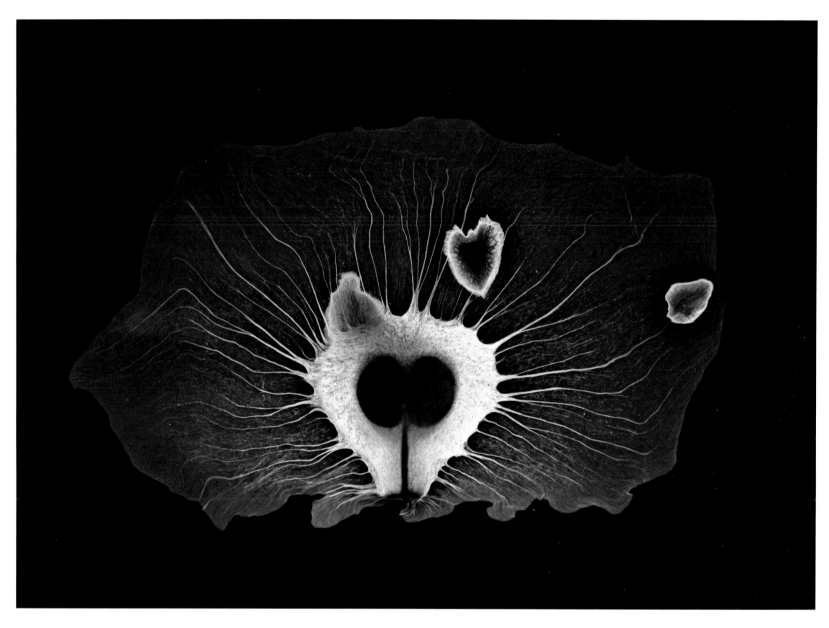

CEDRIC BREGNARD   THIRD   **MARY SUTTON** ···ᐅ   FINALIST

Sorrel and monkey's-comb seeds.   Poppy unfolding.
Geneva Botanical Gardens, Switzerland.

The shape and translucency of these beautiful seeds evoke the energy of life, while the   The colours and textures of this opium poppy (*Papaver somniferum*) were extremely
larger seed's wing protects the smaller ones. Using a combination of shadow and light,   sensuous. I wanted to create the feeling of crumpled velvet and the variety of shades one
I wanted to create the illusion that the light was coming from the heart of the seed.   would see in the pile of the cloth. I often spend time photographing poppy petals because
                    I love their tissue-like quality. On this occasion I gently peeled back the outer casing of the
                    bud and enjoyed working with the crumpled petals. I could see the possibility of creating a
                    beautiful image that would leave the observer wondering what it was.

Wilted hosta portraits.
Vassar College, Poughkeepsie, New York, USA.

These images portray the last stage in the life cycle of the common landscape plant, the hosta. I was struck by their beauty, even in death. Beauty in the garden is sometimes discovered when you least expect it. I had made some successful images of hostas between 2004 and 2007, so I set the goal of carrying out a complete study of them in 2008. I was always attracted to their shapes and the design possibilities their leaves suggested. When autumn came and the frost struck the plants, I checked them every day. I was looking for the right amount of wilting and colour. Eventually, at the beginning of November, they were perfect. Over the next few days I photographed them in various locations and states of degradation.

Nikon D300, 18-200mm zoom and 105mm Micro Nikkor lenses.
Some adjusting of colour was carried out, as well as some darkening around the edges and removal of spots/blemishes.

–*Bright wilted hosta leaves* Brightly coloured, wilted hosta leaves.
–*Torn and wilted leaves* A weather-battered hosta plant.
–*Leaves and stems* Colourful wilted hosta leaves.
–*Blue and white wilted leaves* Hosta leaves that were hit by frost.
–*Wilted hosta* A hosta plant that was hit by frost.
–*Folded leaf* Wilted and folded hosta leaf.

1

4

5

6

🌱 **JACKY PARKER**   FINALIST

A splash of spring colour.
Iver, Buckinghamshire, England.

A single red anemone flower of Anemone de Caen strain (*Anemone coronaria*). This group is a collective name for a race of single-flowered cultivars with five to eight petals in red, blue or white, and which flower in spring. I loved the bright and vibrant colours of these little poppy-like flowers, which, after the long winter months, seemed so welcome in the spring. As a result, I aimed to capture the vibrant colour of this little red flower while using the other coloured anemones as a background.

NIGEL BURKITT ⋯⊱   FINALIST

Mount Cook lily (*Ranunculus lyallii*).
Hooker Valley, Aoraki/Mount Cook National Park, New Zealand.

I was in New Zealand to shoot landscapes and wildlife. Interested in gardens and plants, I had heard about the Mount Cook lily (it's actually a giant alpine buttercup, not a lily!) and was eagerly anticipating finding it. Walking up the Hooker Valley towards Mount Cook, I found the flower in bloom and growing in profusion. The mountain itself made an appropriate backdrop for the shot.

CAROLINE HYMAN FINALIST

Coiled cyclamen seeds.

The seeds were hidden beneath the cyclamen leaves, lying as tightly coiled as springs on the surface of the soil. They appeared to take the shape and elegance of dancers.

KEVIN HOWCHIN ⋯⋗ FINALIST

Reflected reed stems.
Nova Scotia, Canada.

I have admired other photographers' shots of reflected reed stems before, because I enjoy 'as found' natural abstract images. When taking photos, I strive to follow the 'keep it simple' and 'less is more' guidelines and, on this occasion, produced my most minimal – and abstract – result yet.

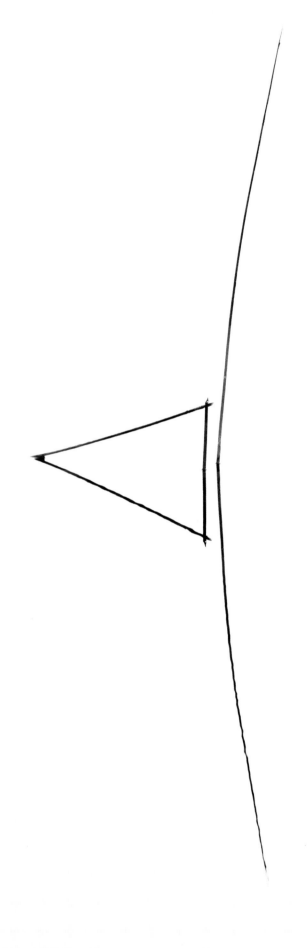

LIZ EVERY

Seed heads and buds.

I am fascinated by the small details of plants and flowers and, when I found and photographed one bud and seed head, I decided to find more and build a collection. The result is this study of the various ingenious, strange and beautiful ways that have developed for plants to wrap or package their seeds or petals.

Canon EOS 40D, 60mm macro lens, f/6.3.
I wanted to photograph all the subjects in the same way – a white background and natural light from the same direction – so that they would all hang together as a group.

1–The caper spurge (*Euphorbia Lathyrus*) seed head.
2–Foxglove (*Digitalis purpurea*) seed heads.
3–Scabiosa 'Cambridge Blue' seed head.
4–*Cephalaria gigantea* bud seed head.
5–*Scabiosa stellata* seed head.
6–Catananche Caerulea bud.

1

2

3

4

5

6

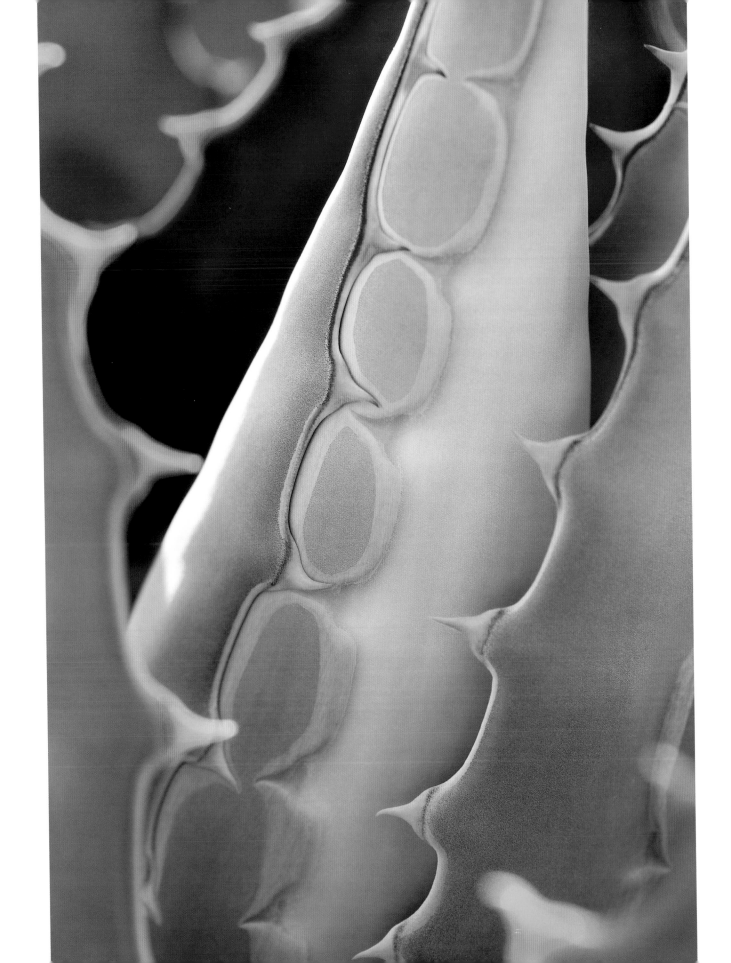

◆··· GEOFF DU FEU   FINALIST

Agave utahensis.
Old Vicarage Gardens, East Ruston, Norfolk, England.

I had been observing this fine specimen on a number of visits throughout the season, and was hoping to capture a graphic image that also showed new leaf formation with a leaf impression still showing on the central rosette. The wonderful spines also had to figure prominently. No tripods are allowed in this garden, so I had to move in close and handhold, bracing my hands against the leaves to prevent camera shake. This literally cost me blood, as the spines are very sharp!

◆ DONALD ROBINSON   FINALIST

Asian lotus.
Phipps Conservatory, Pittsburgh, Pennsylvania, USA.

The Asian lotus originated in Asia more than 3,000 years ago, and carries a rich history in Far Eastern cultures. The species Nelumbo nucifera, known more simply as 'lotus', is an aquatic perennial treasured for its exotic white or pink blossoms and regarded as a symbol of purity and spiritual perfection. The soft light on this particular flower added to its interesting composition.

DAVID MAITLAND FINALIST

Plantscapes.
Garden and meadow, Calne, Wiltshire, England.

Common garden and meadow (weed) plants are often overlooked, yet they remain some of our most beautiful and easily seen plants. Their individual beauty is highlighted in these 'plantscapes' of form and colour. A common blue butterfly (the most widespread blue butterfly in the United Kingdom) is used to place the plants within their habitat and to provide scale and contrast.

Canon flatbed scanner.

I wanted to isolate and emphasise the intricate detail and beautiful form of some of our most common plants, which are frequently ignored or overlooked. I especially like grasses, and wanted to bring them to life by the inclusion of the butterfly, which seems to animate an otherwise static image.

1–*Toadflax* Purple toadflax (*Linaria purpurea*) and common blue butterfly (*Polyommatus icarus*).

2–*Velvet bent* Velvet bentgrass (*Agrostis canina*) and common blue butterfly (*Polyommatus icarus*).

3–*Meadow buttercup* Meadow buttercup (*Ranunculus acris*) and common blue butterfly (*Polyommatus icarus*).

4–*Herb Robert* Herb Robert (*Geranium robertianum*) and common blue butterfly (*Polyommatus icarus*).

5–*Crested dog's tail* Crested dog's tail (*Cynosurus cristatus*) and common blue butterfly (*Polyommatus icarus*).

6–*Creeping soft grass* Creeping soft grass, or hairy knees (*Holcus mollis*) and common blue butterfly (*Polyommatus icarus*).

DAVID THURSTON

Will to live.
Ta Cenc, Gozo, Malta.

A wild thyme, branches bleached as brittle as the bones of a desert carcass, once flourished here, drawing nourishment from its limestone crevice. The shadow of a glorious past, where no bright, timeless lichen has yet ventured, shows in the bareness of stone. One limb struggles on. It signals its implacable determination with fragrant flares of green. This photograph turns out to be one of the most stimulating I have made: the cohabitation of two exquisite and different life forms (actually three, because lichen is half alga and half fungus). It is amazing how excited one can get over what is basically a still life – something that was here yesterday and will be here tomorrow. Here there is no 'decisive moment', yet the scene is charged with meaning.

⚘ SEISHI NAGATSUKA

Water plant.
San Bernardino National Forest, California, USA.

I was enjoying a quiet walk in San Bernardino National Forest, having travelled through the desert in Arizona and California for almost two weeks. It was around 6 o'clock on the warm summer evening when I found a small stream running through the forest. It was so beautiful that I started shooting water plants flowing along the stream using the flash bulb for more interesting light.

VOLKER LAMPE

Calla lily (*Zantedeschia aethiopica*).

I wanted this portfolio to show different aspects of the calla flower. It was more important for me to bring out the tenderness and beauty of the blossoms than to record every last detail. To achieve this, I blended both sharpness and blur within each image.

Hasselblad 500CM, 80mm and 100mm lenses, Ilford FP4 Plus, f/2.8 to f/11.

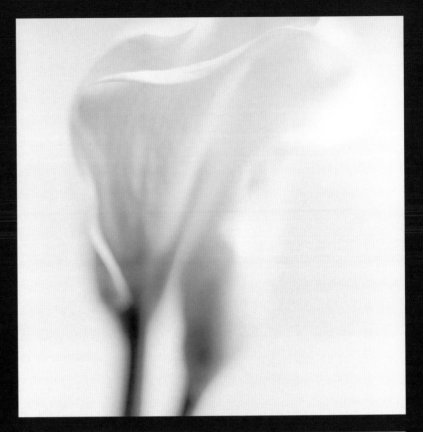

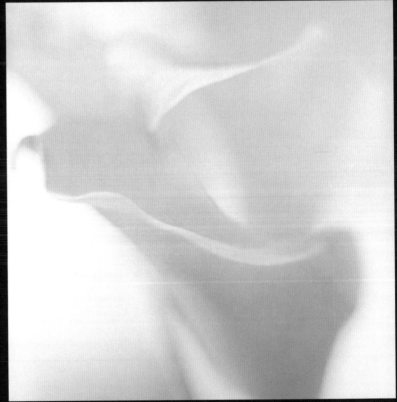

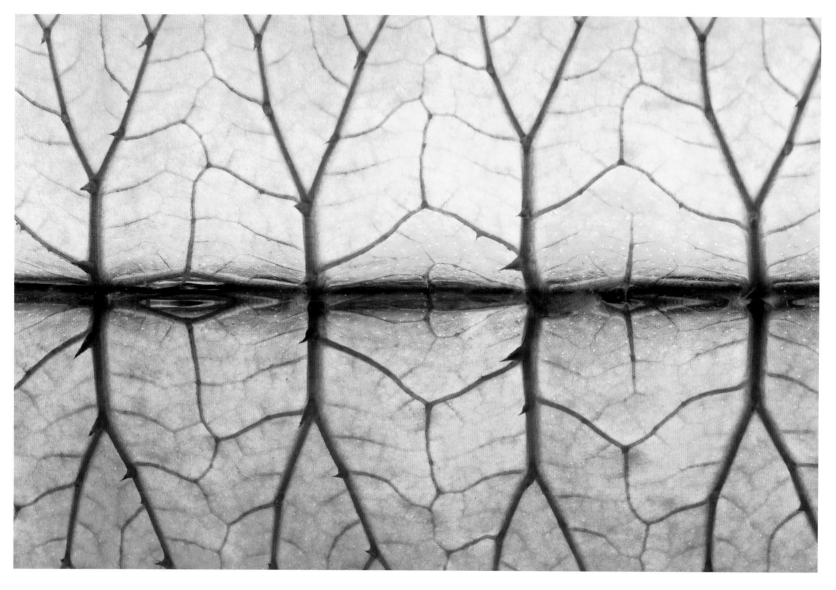

ANDY PHILLIPSON   COMMENDED

DAVID SMITH ⋯⟩   COMMENDED

Victoria amazonica.
Tropical Glasshouse, Royal Botanic Garden, Edinburgh, Scotland.

Moss, *Bryum capillare.*
Stokesley, North Yorkshire, England.

Victoria amazonica is native to the Amazon River, and is the largest of the nymphaea family. The giant pads can reach diameters of three metres and can support the weight of small mammals. The huge flowers start life almost white, before maturing into a delicate pink. I have always been fascinated by giant water lilies, their relationship to each other and to the surface tension of the water which supports their great weight. With this shot I wanted to explore the wonderful symmetries and slightly abstract nature of the capillaries as the sun filtered through them.

Bryum capillare is a common moss that grows unnoticed on stones, walls or paving in most British gardens. Each spring I delight in seeing its nodding, translucent spore capsules glistening in the early morning sunshine, and I hoped to convey this feeling in my photograph. To show them at their best I have photographed the spore capsules life-size as they approach maturity and are still translucent, and I have caught them naturally backlit by the rising sun.

1

2

MICHA PAWLITZKI   <small>COMMENDED</small>

Munich, Germany.

Rollei 6008, Makro Planar 120mm lens, Fuji Velvia 100, 1/2sec.

1–White: The spider lily (*Hymenocallis* x *festalis*).
2–Carmine: The coral lily (*Lilium pumilum*)
3–Red: Gout plant (*Jatropha podagrica*).
4–Yellow: Slipper flower (*Calceolaria species*).
5–Blue: Allium.
6–Purple: The bluebird vine (*Petrea racemosa*).

OLGA JONES COMMENDED

Romantic tulips.
Keukenhof Gardens, Lisse, Holland.

It was early one morning in the Keukenhof Gardens. The tulip displays were captivating, impressive and amazingly colourful. I was attracted to this group of *Tulipa* 'Shirley' which had soft colours, reminding me of ancient silks. After many attempts I captured their sensual softness and romantic character – something I'd been attempting for many years.

WILLIAM PIERSON ⋯⟩ COMMENDED

Bougainvillea with blue wall.
Todos Santos, Baja Sur, Mexico.

This photograph is about the magic of the relationship between colours. I first saw the image from a distance, looking down a dusty Mexican street. The deep pink bougainvillea, illuminated from the side by the intense Mexican light, with the background of blue stucco, was stunning. This flowering shrub, highlighted by the metal-framed window, completed a beautiful composition in colour and form.

RACHEL WARNE   SECOND, AND GPA BEST PORTFOLIO

Autumn study.

wanted to make a study of plants outside their usual environment. The
plants were all gathered from my neighbourhood – from the forest, the
sides of roads and even someone's front garden. Although they are all
dead, photographing them is a way of bringing them back to life. I used
a technique that allowed me to get really close to the fine detail found in
a plant's skeleton.

Scanner.
experimented with the colours and reversed the image, using the
negative instead of the positive image.

1–Sycamore seedling.
2–Dried fern.
3–Grasses.

4–Beech.
5–Aster.
6–Cow parsley.

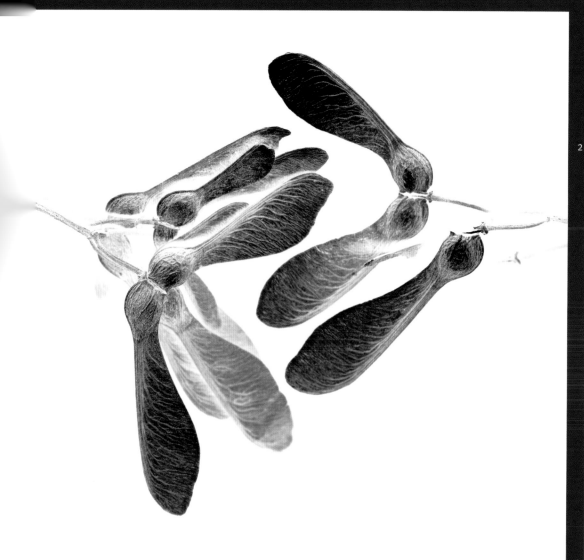

2

3

NOEL BROWNE   FINALIST

Autumn.
Killarney National Park, Co Kerry, Ireland.

The previous autumn I noticed this dead tree stump, but it was too late to photograph that year as the toadstools were already dead. Going back to the same spot at the optimum time the following year, I came across this scene. There was no direct sunlight but the bright conditions were ideal for a subject like this. I was able to get down low to take the shot, and it intrigued me to think that each year, at the same time, these toadstools will spring up on this tree stump and keep on reproducing year after year.

BRENTON WEST   COMMENDED

Phormium.
Rosemoor RHS Garden, Great Torrington, Devon, England.

This image shows the veins and tendons of the Phormium. The colours were amazing and I felt the horizontal lines gave the abstract close-up image a sense of movement.

STEFFIE SHIELDS ···⟩   COMMENDED

Blanket stitch.

An unusually heavy hoarfrost had transformed my garden. There was much to photograph. It was so cold that the frost lingered into the early afternoon when the daylight developed a diffuse pearlised quality and tempted me out again. I came across these hanging *Photinia* x *fraseri* 'Red Robin' leaves (the shrub had been a Mother's Day gift from my daughter). The vivid colours contrasted with the pervasive stark whiteness. Crystals decorated each leaf, and emphasised their form, as if blanket stitch embroidery.

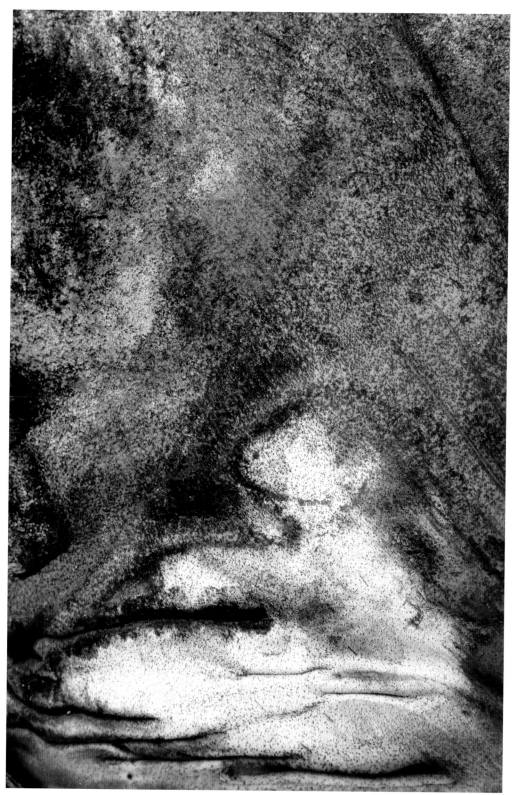

◆···· NORLE COLUSSI   COMMENDED

The art of imperfection III.
The Rio de Janeiro Botanic Garden, Brazil.

The very striking triangle palm (*Neodypsis decaryi*) has leaves
arising from three distinct points around the trunk, forming a
triangle, hence the name. On close observation of its trunk and
petiole it is possible to find the most incredible colours and
patterns, some of which might be a painting on canvas.
Neodypsis decaryi (*Arecaceae*) is classified as Vulnerable on the
IUCN Red List. Native to the Madagascan rainforest and cultivated
in a variety of climates, there are only about 1,000 individuals left in
its native habitat. It is threatened both by fire and the harvesting of
its seeds for export.

TREES

JUDGE'S CHOICE

DENNIS FRATES (p.140)

LONE FALL TREE

This picture made an immediate impression on me when I first saw it. In terms of lighting it has everything, with the dark, moody sky and snow-clad mountains forming a brooding background to the beautifully lit tree, resplendent in its autumn foliage. Dennis has cleverly composed the picture so that the tree is at the intersection of the thirds, resulting in a powerful composition.

Clive Nichols

DENNIS FRATES   First

Lone fall tree.
Ennis, Montana, USA.

This tree was the only one around for miles in this remote area, and its stark beauty appealed to me. It just happened to be in full fall colour the day I passed by. An early fall of snow covered the mountains in the background. I waited for quite some time for the light to arrive at the tree.

CHRIS HUMPHREYS   Second

Enclosure.
'The dark hedges', Bregagh Road, Co Antrim, Northern Ireland.

This beech tree avenue in Co Antrim is known as 'The dark hedges'. It is a very tranquil place where they form a natural arch over the road. The thick tree canopy means that most light enters from the sides, which accentuates the feeling of enclosure. I have passed through many tree-lined roads before, but few have caused me to stop the car without a word and get out with my mouth wide open. There is something very mysterious about this place; I could have stayed all day watching the light change.

🌿 **RAOUL SLATER**   THIRD

Jacaranda (*Jacaranda mimosifolia*).
Pomona, Sunshine Coast, Queensland, Australia.

I was photographing a wild white-headed pigeon in my backyard, and he allowed me to stalk very close, even though my four-year-old boy, Sam, insisted on following me every step of the way. Eventually we were close enough for me to take the 1.4x converter off my 300mm lens and still have a head and shoulders shot. When the pigeon did eventually fly away, this was the image in the viewfinder. The Jacaranda is a South American plant, but has become a symbol of suburban Queensland in Australia. They are frequently planted on streets and around the older style of high-set weatherboard cottages typical of the subtropics here.

GARY STEER   COMMENDED

Evening paperbarks.
Centennial parklands, Sydney, New South Wales, Australia.

A row of broad-leaved paperbark (*Melaleuca quinquenervia*), which are native to the area, and favour moist, even swampy ground. The area was originally known as Lachlan Swamp. Water from this natural freshwater drainage area was channelled via Busby's Bore to the settlement of Sydney. In 1888, Centennial Park was established over the area. I was photographing near the end of the day with the sun behind me. I turned and looked towards the sun and was captivated by the golden backlight on the paperbark. It was irresistible to photograph them.

GARY RAYNER ···> FINALIST

Old tree detail II.
Woodford Golf Course, Essex, England.

The bare, wintry silhouette of this dead tree was a prominent feature
of our local golf course for years. Local legend was that it had been
struck in a storm. As children we called it 'the lightning tree' and
played underneath it, scared that it might fall. Many years later I
found that it had. When I saw it on the ground I was struck by the
texture and lines. I wanted to capture something of the beautiful
grain and rich brown and golden hues in the weathered wood.

⟨··· KIMBERLY BARDOEL   FINALIST

Afloat in the branches.
Sifton Bog, London, Ontario, Canada.

A lone maple leaf appears to float through the air as a momentary burst of light illuminates the surface of the bog to bring this surreal scene to life. I love the mystery and impermanence of this image. This matches the very nature of a bog itself, as all inevitably turn into swamps. This type of wetland is very rare in Ontario, and it is considered to be an ecological jewel in my hometown.

Bogs start out as slow-moving rivers or ponds which are gradually taken over by moss. Under this thick, floating layer of moss is a deep layer of decaying plant matter, called peat. This wetland is home to many carnivorous plants such as horned bladderwort, pitcher plants and sundews.

EDWARD HILL

Greenwich Park, London, England.

My portfolio is a study of trees in winter in Greenwich Park, using my 360-degree photosphere perspective. This perspective allows the viewer to see everything that is visible around a central point, and creates the effect of either looking down on a miniature world or looking up into a surrounding space. I have lived next to the beautiful tree-filled landscape of Greenwich Park for many years. My photospheres illustrate the way that trees, like people, stand rooted on and drawing nourishment from the earth, but are reaching out to and drawing vital force from the heavens.

Nikon D2X.

To give an impression of Greenwich Park, I had in mind to create all-round portraits of some of the mature oaks and 350-year-old chestnut trees, and came close up to them so that I could pan a vertical shot into the canopy as well as a horizontal shot at the trunk. I put these close-up portraits alongside more distant studies of trees that I had created on frosty and snowy mornings.

1–Frosty morning.
2–Spanish chestnut trees (*Castanea sativa*).
3–Spanish chestnut trees (*Castanea sativa*).
4–Snow-covered trees.
5–English oak tree (*Quercus robur*).
6–Holm oak (*Quercus ilex*).

1

2

🌴 **ADAM GIBBS**   <small>COMMENDED</small>

Roots. The western yellow pine (*Pinus ponderosa*).
Zion National Park, Utah, USA.

I loved the way in which the roots spread out across the red sandstone, searching for
moisture. I wanted to emphasise the roots in the foreground, so I placed my camera very
close to them and used a wideangle lens to dramatise the roots' size.

PETE BRIDGWOOD   FINALIST

Lochan na h'Achlaise by torchlight.
Rannoch Moor, Highland, Scotland.

I had hoped to get to this wonderful loch before sunset, but arrived an hour too late. Not to
be deterred in my quest for a magical image in the blackness of darkening twilight, I decided
to create my own illumination using a large, handheld torch.

TONY JONES COMMENDED

Rhus typhina 'Dissecta'.

This photo was taken in February 2008, on a sunny winter's afternoon. I deliberately underexposed the image in order to create the dark, backlit effect. It was impossible to use a tripod so I handheld to achieve just the right viewpoint.

TOM WUNDRAK COMMENDED

Arboreum XVI.
Germany.

Having discovered this scene one misty autumn morning, I was touched by the poetic appearance of these two lonely 'babies' being protected by the small fence around them. The mist that swallowed them created an atmosphere of total isolation and tranquillity, which is reflected in the image's minimalist and symmetrical composition.

RICHARD LOADER

Weeping spruce (*Picea breweriana*) in autumn.
The Arboretum, Ornamental Drive, New Forest, Hampshire, England.

During a visit to the Arboretum I sheltered from a sudden downpour beneath the umbrella-like canopy of a large weeping spruce. While waiting for the rain to stop, I noticed the raindrops on the foliage and the bright, saturated colours of the fallen leaves in the background. The simplicity of the subject attracted me, as did the abstract nature of the image, with the foliage seemingly inverted, yet the raindrops showing the correct orientation. The mass of golden Acer foliage in the background made for a bright foil and helped set the season of the shot.

PAUL DEBOIS

FINALIST

Junction 6 no.1.
M40, Buckinghamshire, England.

Part one of a pair of images, Junction 6 is a 180-degree view of a motorway junction on the M40. The road has been carved through a hillside, with dense woodland planted right up to the border of the motorway. The view has always interested me. I wanted to produce an image that showed the density of traffic travelling through beautiful woodland, highlighting human intervention and the fragile nature of what remains. The image is constructed from 369 individual photographs, randomly arranged to create a sense of disorder. The only constant is the line of the motorway, which is isolated to emphasise the effect of the road through the landscape.

JAMES GUILLIAM   COMMENDED

Woodlands of North Yorkshire.
Ingleton and Clapham, North Yorkshire Dales,
England.

These images were taken during a stroll in the country with my family and seven-month-old puppy. I was travelling light, with just one camera body and one lens. All the images were taken quickly, as I was supposed to be with the family and not taking photographs! The light was silvery, with a weak, pale, watery sun, which highlighted the wet branches of the trees. I wanted to capture the essence of the day, for the viewer to smell the woodland and feel the cool, fresh air.

1

2

Canon EOS-1Ds Mk III, 24-105mm L f/4 lens, f/11, f/8 and f/6.3.
This series of images was picked from around 50 shots taken on one afternoon. It was created using slow shutter speeds that varied from 1/2sec to one second long, at apertures which governed this, while moving the handheld camera around during the exposure.

MICHA PAWLITZKI   COMMENDED

American aspen trees (*Populus tremuloides*) in first light.
Manti-La Sal National Forest, Utah, USA.

It was simply the incredible autumnal colours that attracted me to this scene.

CHRISTINA BOLLEN/GAP PHOTOS   FINALIST

Frosted fallen leaves.
Harlow Carr RHS Garden, Harrogate, Yorkshire, England.

The sweet gum tree (*Liquidambar styraciflua*) is a native of North America and renowned for its intense autumn colours. The autumn of 2008 was unusually frosty in the UK; it was visually spectacular as the autumn colours and textures were given an extra dimension with the addition of sparkling ice crystals. Frost is very delicate and I had to be careful not to touch or move any of the leaves, even if I had wanted to for artistic purposes!

ADAM TRIGG

Shadows in the evening light.
Ashridge Park, Hertfordshire, England.

I had noticed the strong shadows created by the golden light while driving past one evening, and returned on foot to take the photograph the next day. A low viewpoint was used to emphasise the strong shadows among the common beech trees (*Fagus sylvatica*). This made using a tripod quite difficult, but the camera could be held steady by using the surrounding trees as support.

PETER O'HARE

On fire.
Itchingwood Common, Surrey, England.

The research laboratory where I work is situated in a place where we get beautiful sunsets; but I had never seen the colours as at the end of this day. The woods were aglow and, seeing it unfold, I had to stop science and capture it. I had only a little time, but needed to capture as much of the shafts of light as I could, while hoping they would not disappear. Angled for as much depth as possible, I wanted to transform a pleasant view into an inspiration.

WILDLIFE IN THE GARDEN

JUDGE'S CHOICE

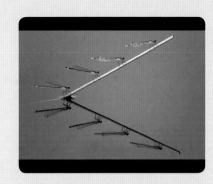

COLIN VARNDELL (p.162)

DAMSELFLIES ON
GARDEN POND

Calm, ripple-free water mirrors emergent grasses and

reeds, but in this stunning shot we have so much more.

When photographing any mobile wildlife it is always a

gamble whether to take what you first see and move on,

or to wait for a better composition. Here, Colin Varndell's

wait paid off when four damselflies spaced themselves out

equidistantly on a dry reed – in perfect light.

Heather Angel

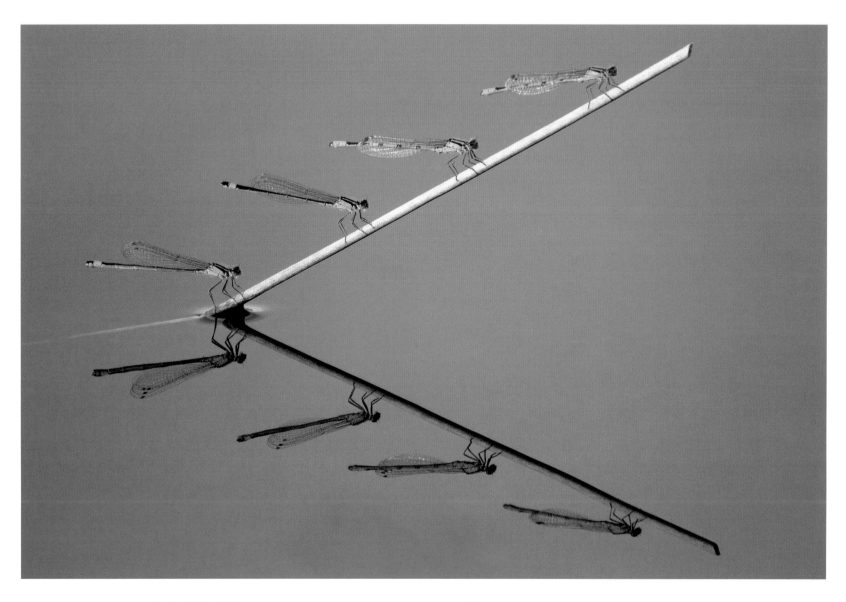

🌱 **COLIN VARNDELL** FIRST

Damselflies on garden pond.
Netherbury, Dorset, England.

I have always been fascinated with dragonflies and damselflies and spend time
photographing them every year. In this instance, I was inspired by the way they all settled
on the reeds in the same direction due to the gentle breeze. I set up my tripod and seat and
waited. Most of the time there were so many insects on the reeds that they looked untidy.
But after a wait of a couple of hours I noticed these four, symetrically positioned on this
reed. The top two damselflies are common blues (*Enallagma cyathigerum*) the lower two are
blue-tailed damselflies (*Ischnura elegans*). As with many nature subjects, patience was the
key with this shot. I carry a fold-up seat on my camera bag for such occasions and used this
to sit and wait for the right moment.

MAGDALENA WASICZEK   SECOND

Summer shower.
Trzebinia/Malopolska region, Poland.

Polyommatus icarus is the most common butterfly in the part of Poland where I live; it's around from May until the end of September. This June day started off warm and sunny, but a summer shower caught me out while I was photographing. I managed a few shots before my 'model' escaped to find a safe place.

JOHN PENBERTHY   THIRD

Gulls on glasshouse roof.
The Royal Botanic Gardens, Kew, Surrey, England.

Little gulls (*Larus minutus*) are a common winter visitor to Kew. With their winter plumage and distinctive red legs and feet, they look similar to a tern. Making his first visit to Kew, my seven-year-old nephew spotted the gulls on the roof as we made our way up the stairs. He thought it was hilarious to be able to see the gulls' bottoms. I liked his laughter and the simple colour contrasts.

RAOUL SLATER   FINALIST

Wattlebird on forest grass tree (*Xanthorrhoea latifolia*).
Pomona, Sunshine Coast, Queensland, Australia.

The two grass trees were growing at my neighbour's gate, and they sent up two beautiful, parallel flower spikes. I set up a hide and photographed the honeyeaters that came to feed on the copious nectar. This wattlebird was just long enough to reach from one spike to the other, giving the image a pleasing tension. I almost never photograph a wildlife subject against a blue sky, but the project called for bold, clean images, so I broke one of my own rules.

PAUL KEENE FINALIST

Garden tiger moth (*Arctia caja*) close-up.
Amersham, Buckinghamshire, England.

The garden tiger was a common moth when I was young and I would often see the 'woolly bear' caterpillars crawling across the footpath. However, like most moth species, they are much more rare now. The caterpillars feed on nettles (as do many of our favourite butterflies) so it is worthwhile helping them out by keeping a rough, uncultivated patch in your garden. The striking warning colours and distinct patterns make an interesting abstract image.

SARAH-FIONA HELME ⋯⋯➔ FINALIST

Summer stripes.
Kingfisher Cottage, Stonehouse, South Lanarkshire, Scotland.

Most of the flowers in my garden I grow from seed and I choose varieties that attract beneficial insects such as this gazania. I was drawn by the bright, bold colours and stripes of both the host and the hoverfly. I wanted to show how they complement one another, so I decided to take the shot looking down from above.

◁⋯ OLEGAS KURASOVAS   FINALIST

Diamonds on 'fur'.
Vilnius, Lithuania.

The morning light and dew sparkled on this butterfly's 'fur'.

⋆ ALISTAIR CAMPBELL   COMMENDED

Patience.

A crab spider, having taken on the colour of the flower, waits patiently for its next meal. The spider stayed on the same flower for several weeks. It took a long time for the spider to accept me and let me get this close. At x4 the end of the lens is within two inches of the subject. I was inspired by how the yellows of the flower and crab spider seem to become one, making the spider almost part of the flower and virtually invisible.

† ALBERT ROBB COMMENDED

Crow on nest.
Church Farm, Suffolk, England.

I find crows fascinating and have many images of them. This one was on its nest in my in-laws' garden, and the winter sun shining through the tree branches enhanced the mood. I kept one branch in focus for depth. Most photographers like to take sharp images, but I prefer the effect of soft focus. My main love, however, is trying to capture light, in all its different forms.

CHRISTINE WHATLEY ··⟩ FINALIST

Fish at Sir Harold Hillier Gardens.
Romsey, Hampshire, England.

The way the sun shone through the cloudy water, casting shadows below the fish, gave the surreal impression they were floating above the water. The colour of the cloudy water complemented the colours of the fish perfectly. I chose an area where there was as little distraction as possible from shadows or ripples, to result in a very simple composition where all there is to see is the fish and their shadows on the cloudy water below.

170

NINA JONSSON FINALIST

Insects in my Norwegian garden.

As an ecologist, I find common garden insects beautiful.
Without magnification, though, the viewer cannot study their
details. Therefore, I created this portfolio to raise awareness of
their characteristics.

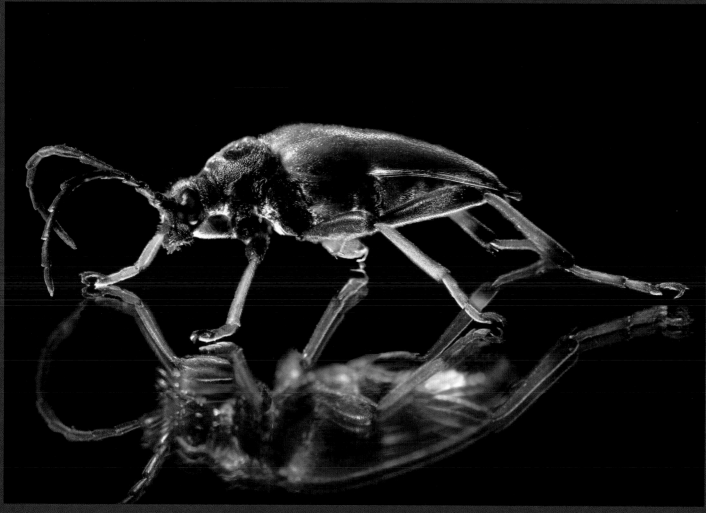

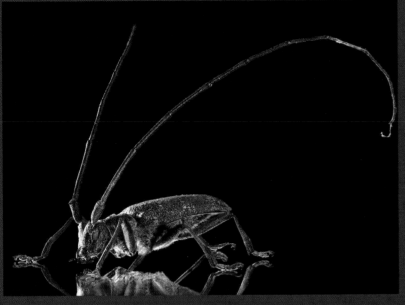

3

4

5

6

Canon EOS 5D Mk II.

I am interested in the sharpness of photographs. Therefore I was keen to use f/10 rather than f/32 to increase maximum sharpness at the point of focus. To compensate for the lack of depth of field, I made several exposures to cover the depth of the whole insect. These were overlaid, and the blurry areas from each one erased. The result is a picture where each of the points of focus is visible.

1–Common house fly (*Musca domestica*).
2–*Anoplodera rubra*.
3–*Ecyrus arcuatus*.
4–Wasp.
5–*Bombus* sp. Humblebee.
6–Bush-cricket (*Tettigonia viridissima*).

FERGUS GILL   FINALIST

COLIN VARNDELL   COMMENDED

Goldfinch (*Carduelis carduelis*) feeding on a teasel (*Dipsacus fullonum*).

Young starlings fighting.
Netherbury, Dorset, England.

I took this photograph on Christmas morning a couple of years ago. The day was bitterly cold, with temperatures several degrees below zero. Because of this, food was very scarce and a pair of goldfinches arrived in the garden to feed on some teasels we grow every year. This image shows one of the goldfinches feeding on a frozen teasel plant, pausing momentarily to look at the camera.

I noticed these young starlings (*Sturnus vulgaris*) coming to our garden bird table in midsummer. They seemed to spend more time fighting than they did feeding, so I set up a small hide nearby and waited for the action. The camera shot at nine frames per second in order to capture the moment.

CHRIS MINIHANE   FINALIST

Bug on thistle bush.
Karen, Kenya.

This very colourful beetle was laying her eggs on a thistle bush.
I took this shot because I'd never seen anything like this before,
and was fascinated not only by the fact that I'd noticed this small
beetle, but also by her incredible shyness. It was very difficult to get
anywhere near her. I had to carefully walk up to her and simply stand
for several minutes, moving bit by bit until I could get a bit of her face
in the shot. It was very windy and she would turn away from me if I
got too close, or if I moved an inch, so this was a lucky shot indeed.

KRZYSZTOF TRUSZ   COMMENDED

Bumblebee in the grass.

The aim of this photograph is to show a bumblebee from the
perspective of another insect. In order to get the result I was after
I had to crawl around on the ground for some time. I got dirty, but I
got the shot, too!

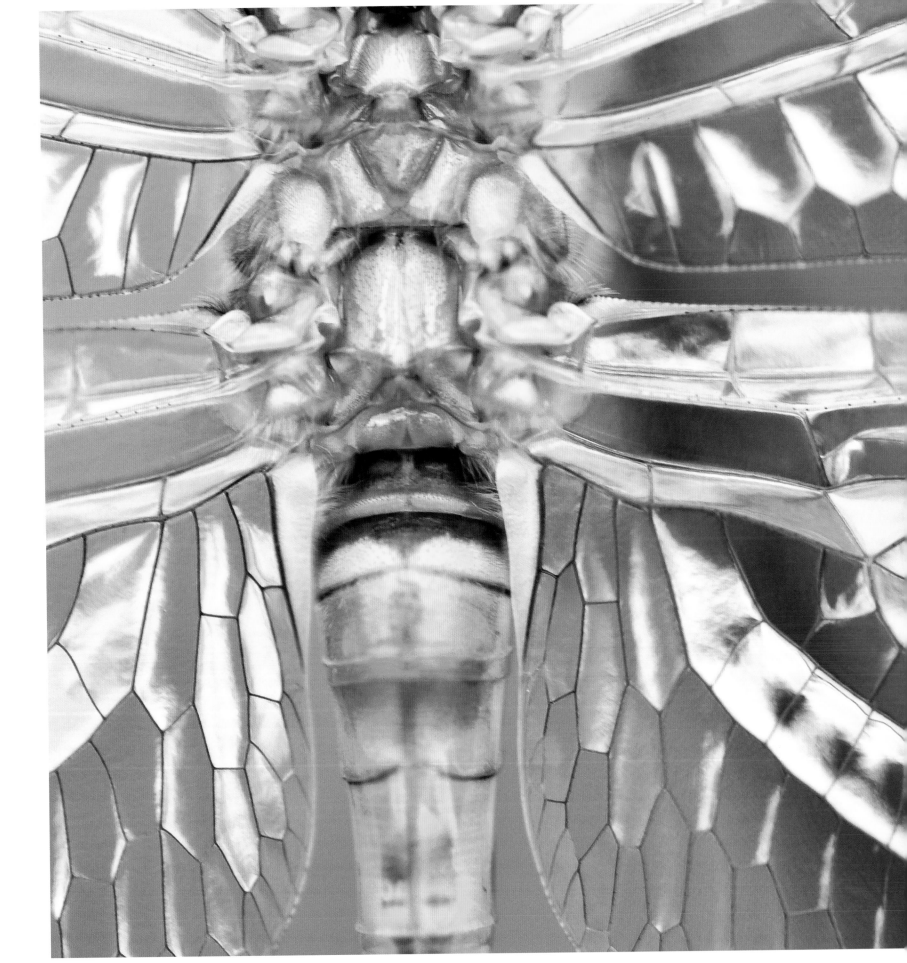

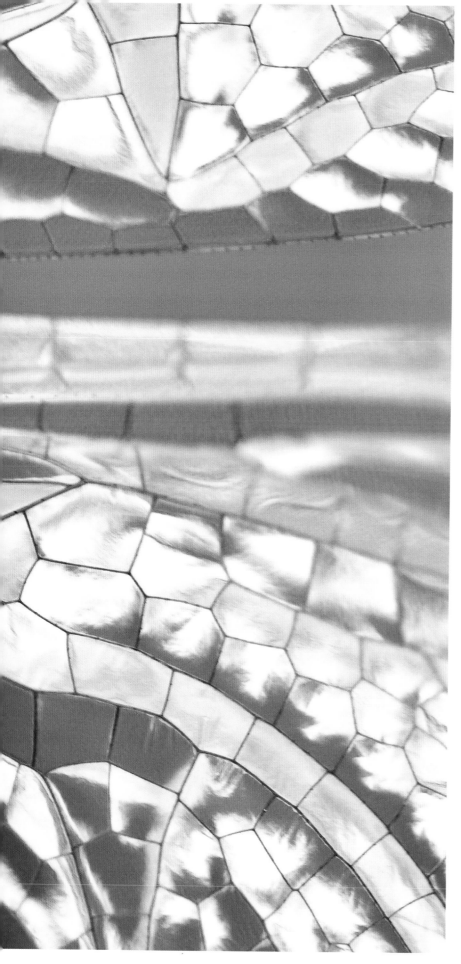

JASON SMALLEY   FINALIST

Wings of newly emerged dragonfly.
River Ribble, Preston, Lancashire, England.

I was drawn to the fragility of the wings that would soon power this large insect predator.
To capture the image, I had to stalk slowly through the pond-side vegetation without
disturbing the dragonfly.

PATRICIA FENN   COMMENDED

JANE LEWIS   COMMENDED

Smiling tree frog on cloche.

Poised for action.
Turkey.

This little common tree frog, *Hyla arborea* (Anura), seemed to enjoy having his picture taken and posed nicely on our garden cloche. I got on my hands and knees and crept closer, taking a shot every couple of inches. I tried to make each one count as I didn't know when he might hop off, but he seemed to be quite interested in the camera. I thought after he was probably fascinated at his own reflection in the lens. Garden wildlife is quite fascinating. I get the chance to see the complete life-cycle of many creatures from dragonflies to wild birds and take a great deal of pleasure in encouraging them by planting and arranging their natural habitat, providing food and nesting materials when they are scarce, and photographing their progression and reproduction.

During a holiday in Turkey I became aware of some sort of insect frantically flitting between the Cosmos flowers in the garden attached to a small roadside cafe. It was the first time I had seen the aptly named hummingbird hawk moth (*Macroglossum stellatarum*). From the way the moth hovers in mid-air to feed on flowers it is easy to mistake it for a hummingbird. The speed of movement meant that it was not easy to focus but I was pleased to capture this image which clearly shows the moth's long proboscis just before it is uncoiled and used to extract nectar.

CRAIG CHURCHILL FINALIST

Fieldfare in the snow.
Brackley, Northamptonshire, England.

A late snowfall in March resulted in the winter thrushes desperately looking for food. The hawthorn (*Crataegus laevigata*) bush at the end of the drive held a few remaining berries and, as the snow fell, I released the shutter, hoping to catch the slow-falling flakes around the fieldfare (*Turdus pilaris*). It was a shot I had envisaged taking for a long time but a lack of snow had always prevented it. Thankfully the late winter snowfall changed that!

VALERIE McANINCH COMMENDED

New snow.
Buck Creek State Park, Springfield, Ohio, USA.

During a severe snowstorm last winter I loaded up my gear and headed to the local garden in our state park. I had hoped the white-out conditions would make for some interesting abstract with the plant life and stone walls. I made a few exposures but none that really excited me. I started to leave before the roads became impassable, when a flock of English sparrows descended like a cloud in the bushes. They didn't stay long but I managed to get two shots. Needless to say, I fell in love with this one and it has become one of the favourites in my bird portfolio.

YOUNG INTERNATIONAL GARDEN PHOTOGRAPHER OF THE YEAR

JUDGE'S CHOICE

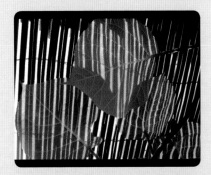

HANNAH BAYNE (p.189)

KIWI TREE IN MY GARDEN

This intimate and striking area of backlit and overlapping Kiwi Tree leaves was well spotted and captured. The freshness of the zingy greens combined with the fragments of red against the dramatic stripes of the shading canes has resulted in a sparkling photograph – a lively graphic image that could also be successfully translated into a variety of media.

Laura Giuffrida

YOUNG
INTERNATIONAL
GARDEN
PHOTOGRAPHER
OF THE YEAR

WINNER

EPSON®
EXCEED YOUR VISION

◄┅┅ **KAT WATERS** (age 15)　　　　　　　First *Plant Portraits*

Purple haze.
Cherkley Court, Surrey, England.

I'd been scouring the gardens at Cherkley Court, in Surrey, for interesting subjects to
photograph. I have an interest in macro photography and botanical subjects are always well
suited. I don't usually experiment with Photoshop effects; however, I feel that in this case,
the use of radial blur enhances the natural explosive look of the bloom.

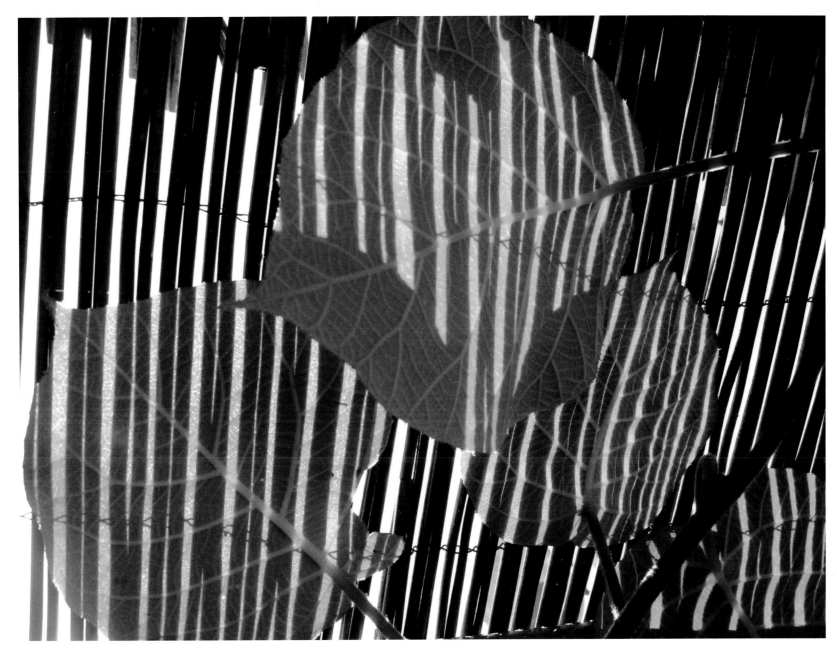

DAZYL YOUNG (age 14)　　　SECOND *WILDLIFE IN THE GARDEN*

HANNAH BAYNE (age 11)　　　THIRD *TREES*

A squirrel's gaze.
Scotland.

Kiwi tree (*Actinidia deliciosa*) in my garden.
Pinsou, Aleu, Ariège, France.

When I first fell in love with photography I only took pictures of still subjects, such as plants and flowers, then later I discovered the wonderful world of wildlife. There is much more involved in photographing wildlife. It requires careful planning, determination, commitment and the desire to make a photograph that captures the moment. During one of my vacations, we had our first family picnic, and I saw this squirrel climbing a tree not very far from us. I waited for it to be in the perfect spot, where the green background would complement the subject. The day ended with a smile for me.

I took this photograph because I liked the shades on the leaves, the contrast between the green and the black, and the lines. To be closer to the leaves, I climbed on a chair and I took several shots from different angles.

🔱 **ESME MORISHIMA** (age 14)   FINALIST *WILDLIFE IN THE GARDEN*

Bonjour.
Ile de Ré, France.

It was the first day of my holiday on the Ile de Ré, and it was raining, so all the snails
(or escargots) were out. I have a lot of photos of this particular snail, but this one was
especially endearing; I just love how much expression and character he is displaying.
Pretty impressive, for a mollusc.

🌱 **JOE GOLDMAN** (age 14)   FINALIST *GARDEN VIEWS*

Autumn bench.
Epsom, Surrey, England.

I was in the garden taking photographs with my father's camera. The lichen on the bench
caught my eye, as I had wanted to get some nice artistic shots of our garden.

JACK ASHWORTH (age 11)   FINALIST *WORLD BOTANIC GARDENS*

HOLLY HOLSTON (age 14)   FINALIST *GARDEN VIEWS*

Maggot's eye view.
RHS Wisley, Surrey, England.

Moss.

I was intrigued by the wickerwork sculpture of a pear, placed just next to the orchard, and realised that the view out through the hole was at just the right angle to catch the lines of trees disappearing towards the horizon. I crawled inside the sculpture and tried to get the best angle possible.

This moss had developed on the rooftop outside of my window. It was covered in dew and sparkling in the sunlight.

🌱 **BEN MIESZKOWSKI** (age 14) COMMENDED *PEOPLE IN THE GARDEN*

Eliot.
The Royal Botanic Gardens, Kew, Surrey, England.

How do you keep cool on a hot summer's day? A group of friends and I were on a school trip to Kew, when my friend Eliot thought jumping through a sprinkler would be an amusing way to cool down. One of my favourite photographers is Nils Jorgensen, and I like how he captures people in his photography. I wanted my photograph to be in a similar style.

194

✝ **JAMIE GOULD** (age 12)   COMMENDED *PEOPLE IN THE GARDEN*

The smoking gardener.
Langworth, Lincolnshire, England.

My granddad, Arnold Hadwin, was having a bonfire, burning some leaves from his garden.
I saw him smoking his pipe, and he was producing almost as much smoke as the fire! I like
this picture because it shows him enjoying his pipe and his garden. He says it is the only
place he is allowed to smoke these days.

JAMIE UNWIN (age 13)　　　　FINALIST *PLANT PORTRAITS*　　　**BRIDIE HUSBAND** (age 13)　　COMMENDED *WILDLIFE IN THE GARDEN*

Chinese lantern *Physalis alkekengi* var. *franchetii*.

Swallowtail caterpillar.
Ranworth Broad Visitors' Centre, Norfolk, England.

I knew my mum had a collection of Chinese lanterns in one of the borders in the front garden, so one day I decided to have a closer look. I was struck by the detail they possessed in their tiny, intricate veins, so felt they had real potential for a photograph. This example was illuminated by the winter sunlight, which highlighted the attractive pattern of veining and enhanced the unique but beautiful shape of the fragile pod.

The caterpillar had beautiful markings and stood out from the stem, so I tried to make it the main focus of the photograph. By taking the picture from the side it meant the stem ran across the photo diagonally, which makes it more dynamic.

🌱 **SAM ROWLEY** (age 14) ···}> ···}> FINALIST *PLANT PORTRAITS*

COMMENDED *GARDEN VIEWS*

Glowing leaves.
WWT London Wetland Centre, England.

As I was walking back to the car park, I spotted out of the corner of my eye a pair of glowing leaves on a birch tree at the North American section of the WWT London Wetland Centre. The leaves were surrounded by shaded trees and the sunlight just reached the leaves to really make them stand out for a picture. I underexposed the shot to exaggerate the darkness of the shadows in the background.

Evening door.
Åre, Sweden.

On a skiing holiday in Sweden, I was photographing moose in the town of Åre, when I saw this striking, evening-light door with distinctive contrasting shadows of a birch tree in front of it. I stood out of the way of the sun's shadows on the barn door so only the birch trees' shadows would show, and not mine.

Yellowhammer prance.
Åre, Sweden.

I spotted this yellowhammer when I went on a short walk around the town of Åre in
Sweden. It was jumping towards seeds under a birdfeeder in a woman's front garden.

BEN MIESZKOWSKI (age 14)   COMMENDED *GARDEN VIEWS*

PETER CURRY (age 12) ⋯⋗   COMMENDED *TREES*

Sweet chestnuts.
The Royal Botanic Gardens, Kew, Surrey, England.

This sweet chestnut was emerging from its prickly case. This is a different view of Kew, taken at ground level. I enjoy experimenting with depth of field – I also like getting up close to my subjects.

Tree reflection on path.
Kröller-Müller Museum, Hoge Veluwe National Park, The Netherlands.

It was a wet day in the Sculpture Garden of the Kröller-Müller Museum, and the trees were waving in the water. I tried to bring together the contrast between the lawn, the reflection, and the perspective of the sculpture running into the distance.

KAT WATERS (age 15) COMMENDED *TREES*

High and dry.
Box Hill, Surrey, England.

I was creeping around in the undergrowth at Box Hill and on the lookout for something to photograph. Despite it being April, I came across this dead leaf still hanging onto the tree and looking very autumnal. The light was fading so this shot took several attempts, but I refused to leave the scene without a good image to show for my pains. I liked the way the leaf had curled up and formed an almost sculptural shape. The soft evening light (although fading with frustrating rapidity) complimented the spiralling form of the leaf.

ISABEL GARBETT (age 14) COMMENDED *TREES*

Autumn maple.
Westonbirt Arboretum, Gloucestershire, England.

This mature *Acer palmatum* looked so lush and vibrant I just had to take a picture. It reminds me of a tree from Narnia.

ROSIE TURNER (age 15)   FINALIST *TREES*

Where my heart lies.
Tebay, Cumbria, England.

I spotted Heart Wood in Cumbria while driving past on the M6. I wondered why everyone else could rush past in their cars and ignore something so pretty. I had to have something to remember it by. The UK is full of sites and wonders that so many people fail to take notice of. Everyone is in a rush now and I wish more people would stop to appreciate beautiful landscapes such as this one. Although I have a lot of photographs from my travels, I always remember this as my favourite because it never fails to make me smile.

DOMINIC JONES (age 15) ···▶   FINALIST *TREES*

Ray of dawn.
Little Houghton, Northamptonshire, England.

I intended upon taking photographs of the sunrise early one morning. Instead I awoke to a thick mist with appealing sunrays. I wanted to create an interesting shot of these beams coming through the branches of this mature Wellingtonia (*Sequoiadendron giganteum*). I also knew I needed a wide depth of field so I shot with a small aperture.

TECHNICAL INFORMATION

HEATHER EDWARDS (p.3)
The secret garden.

Nikon D80, Nikon 18-70mm lens, f/13.

PAUL DEBOIS (p.5)
Gregg Wallace.

Kodak Pro/SLRc, 105mm Sigma Macro lens, f/5.6.
I wanted to use natural lighting as much as possible – the only help came from a large reflector. Even though the photo was taken early in the morning, the sun was quite harsh, so we had to time shots as clouds passed overhead, softening hard shadow.

HILARY FORSTER (p.9)
Informal vegetable-growing.

Samsung Digimax V4, Schneider Varioplan Zoom 7.7-23.1mm lens.
I took the shot at an oblique angle using the vehicles and bikes to frame the image and provide scale comparison to bring out the diminutive size of the garden. I framed it to exclude the surrounding buildings and to show the proximity of the garden to the road.

JONATHAN BERMAN (pp.22–23)
In Tresco Abbey Gardens.

Canon D60, DIY infrared sensor conversion.
I used a sensor filter that was sensitive to infrared (from Life Pixel). Digital infrared images often lack contrast so I undertook contrast enhancements using Photomatix Pro for general tone control and Photoshop CS3 for local control using layers and masks. The image was desaturated then toned.

SAM STYLES (p.24)
The Privy Garden in snow.

Canon EOS 350D, Sigma 17-70mm lens at 17mm setting, f/19.
Under cover of snow, form and shape become more important. Snow is tricky to capture and needs to be overexposed otherwise it comes out grey instead of white. The image was cropped at the top and bottom to produce a letterbox effect.

CLAIRE TAKACS (p.25)
Spring at King John's Lodge.

Canon EOS-1Ds, 70-200mm lens, f/5.6.
I moved around the garden, following where the light was interesting. With this photograph, I stood back from a distance and used my telephoto lens to zoom in and create this composition. I hope it reflects my response to the magic of the garden in the early morning light.

KURT TONG (p.34)
Birdcages.

Linhof Master Technika, Kodak Portra 160NC.
The juxtaposition of the real trees with the caged birds against the fake bamboo and free birds appealed to me. The colours were quite muted except for the plastic cages.

CLAIRE TAKACS (p.26)
Goegap Nature Reserve, Northern Cape, South Africa.

Canon EOS-1Ds, 17-40mm lens, f/13.
I used a wideangle lens, and a landscape format, as I wanted to lead the eye towards the background, where the road went off into the distance. The scale of the landscape required maximum depth of field, hence the small aperture.

SOULA ZAVACOPOULOS (p.35)
Outside in.

Nikon D70, 18-50mm lens at 25mm setting, f/4.

SUE STUBBS (p.27)
Gardens are for pleasure.

Canon EOS-1D Mk III, Canon EF 24-70mm f/2.8L lens, f/22.
I was on top of the stairs, looking out over the garden to the sunset. I wanted depth of field and a fast shutter speed, and the light was getting low. Changing to a faster ISO allowed me to capture the flowing grasses and retain the depth of field.

SIMON GRIFFITHS (p.36)
The Leeming garden.

Canon EOS-1D Mk II, 24-70mm lens, f/10.
I had photographed this garden before, so was familiar with it and knew I wanted to achieve some more unusual views of the house and garden.

NICOLA STOCKEN TOMKINS (p.32)
Winter dawn.

Hasselblad 503CW, 120mm lens, Fuji Velvia 50, f/32.
I had walked for miles through the woodland stopping at times to turn a full 360 degrees before choosing this spot, confident the sun would break through. I pushed the film one stop to allow for maximum depth of field as it was rather dark in the wood.

SIMON GRIFFITHS (p.37)
Cruden Farm.

Canon EOS-1Ds Mk II, 24-70mm lens, f/13.
I aimed to arrive as early as possible in order to capture the magical early morning light.

NICHOLAS HASTINGS-WINCH (p.33)
The circle.

Nikon D700, Nikon 24-85mm lens, f/11.
After visiting the area several times I realised that the sun would rise behind the yews and shooting into the sun would add colour. A hard frost during winter made the scene even more atmospheric.

MARY KOCOL (p.40)
Lilac landscape.

Diana toy camera, cloudy setting, Fuji 400H film.
I chose the Diana camera for its ephemeral, dreamlike effect on the landscape. I love the camera's selective soft-focus quality.

YOSHKO PALENIK (p.41)
Morning walk.

Olympus E-500, Olympus 14-45mm lens at 25mm setting, f/6.3.

ANDREA JONES (p.46)
Lurie Gardens.

Kodak DCS Pro SLR/n, Schneider Super-Angulon PC 28mm f/2.8 lens.
I was inspired by the contrast between the linear architecture and the soft meadow planting.

DENNIS FRATES (p.42)
Japanese gardens in fall.

Canon EOS-1Ds Mk III, Canon 24-105mm f/4 IS lens, f/14.
The lack of wind allowed me to make the long exposure needed. I took three vertical images of this scene and then stitched them in Photoshop. I also used a polariser to saturate the colours.

ANDREA JONES (p.47)
Thomas Jefferson's Monticello Gardens.

Kodak Pro SLR/n.
I arrived before dawn and waited for the sun to rise. When the light appeared through the mist it created a magical glow of colour. I removed an unsightly light fitting beneath the tree in Photoshop and enhanced the image using curves.

ROB WHITWORTH (p.43)
Early summer in a Wiltshire garden.

Hasselblad XPan II, Fuji Velvia 50.

MATTHEW BISHOP (p.50)
The Alpine House.

Canon EOS 400D, Canon EF-S18-55mm f/3.5-5.6 lens, ISO 100, 1/320sec.
A second underexposed shot was also taken at 1/1000sec and merged with the original in Photoshop to increase the dynamic range of the shot and thus better capture the glow of the grasses and Alpine House in the sunlight.

JASON LISKE (p.44)
Water garden.

Canon EOS 5D, Canon 17-40mm lens, f/11.
My approach here was to catch the garden at first light, angling to pull the viewer into the space. One might imagine walking down and experiencing the pool and vista for a morning swim.

ANDY SMALL (p.51)
Castle Rock, Kirstenbosch.

Nikon D300, Nikon DX 17-55mm lens.
I knew the shot I wanted from researching earlier, so waited for the sun to drop below the mountain. I worked quickly, trying different compositions with the Strelitzia as the foreground.

MARTYN GREENHALGH (p.45)
Garden ornament behind a screen of foliage.

Rolleiflex 2.8E, Kodak TMAX 100, light yellow filter.
To maintain the feeling of the delicate tracery of the foliage against the solidity of the urn, and also the quality of the light, precise control of exposure was necessary to retain detail in the delicate highlights and shadows.

NIKKI DE GRUCHY (p.52)
Simulation.

Canon EOS 5D, Canon EF 24-70mm f/2.8L lens at 24mm setting.
Converted to black and white to heighten the graphic nature of the image.

JUNE KINGSBURY (p.53)
Leaf lily.

Canon EOS 40D, 18-55mm lens.
I took several close-up images of the leaf and the goldfish which kept surfacing and creating rings in the water, but it was only when I stood back that the whole grid pattern formation became obvious.

BAPI CHAKRABORTY (p.58)
Conservation.

Canon EOS 40D.
This is a high dynamic range image, made from three frames taken at different exposures, combined and tone-mapped in Photoshop. Various subtle masked layers of tone, curves, saturation and dodge/burn were then applied to capture the original mood when shooting the subject.

DAMIAN GILLIE (p.54)
Bird of paradise flower (*Strelitzia reginae*).

Canon EOS 5D Mk II, 28mm lens, f/9.5.

DANNY BEATH (p.59)
The Climatron.

Nikon FE2, 20mm anamorphic lens, Fuji Velvia, f/11, tripod.

DAMIAN GILLIE (p.55)
Ficus species and a black-bold *Philodendron* leaf.

Canon EOS 5D Mk II, 35mm lens, f/4.5.
The wide aperture and the closeness of the foreground leaf created a soft edge, which contrasts with the hardness of the leaf behind it.

JOHN QUINTERO (p.60)
Palm House.

Nikon D2X, Nikkor 24-120mm f/3.5-5.6 IF-ED AF-S VR zoom lens.
I used a polarising filter to enhance the contrast and avoid reflections on the glass building. The camera was set up to time delay and a tripod was also used to ensure a sharp image. Converted to black and white using Adobe Lightroom.

DAVID MAITLAND (p.56)
Palm House bracket.

Canon EOS-1Ds Mk II.

JEFF EDEN (p.61)
Palm House at sunrise.

Nikon D300, f/5.
This picture came about thanks to obsessive weather report watching in the middle of winter, and the setting of three alarms (alas, I am not a morning person). I did a couple of recces to work out the composition of the final shot.

CAROLINE AMES (p.57)
Silent odyssey.

Olympus SP-500UZ, f/2.8.
Before taking the photograph I walked round the lake studying the Glasshouse from all angles and various levels. I wanted to make the most of the building and its reflection in the water, and this seemed to be achieved best by standing close to the rear elevation.

JUNE KINGSBURY (p.62)
The Eden Project.

Minolta DiMAGE Xt.
What I liked about this image was the relationship between the pitcher plants in the foreground, which frame the biome, and the darker green of the plants on the top bank, which are also reflected in the water.

STEVE REW (p.63)
In front of the Palm House.

Canon G7.
Processed in Apple Aperture to adjust mid tone levels and sharpen.

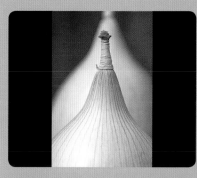

JO WHITWORTH (p.70)
Prize-winning onion 'Kelsae'.

Nikon D200, 105mm macro lens, f/4.
This particular onion stood out for its graphic simplicity, with its twine binding complementing its own stripes, and the larger onion framing it behind. I made the sepia image to link this photo, taken in the 21st century, to its history dating back for generations.

THAMER AL-TASSAN (p.64)
Nan Lian Garden Bridge.

Canon EOS 450D, Sigma 10-20mm lens, f/4.
I used a wideangle lens in order to get more perspective on the bridge.

RICHARD FREESTONE (p.71)
Half-used garlic bulb.

Canon EOS-1Ds Mk II.
The pure black background was added digitally.

ANDREA JONES (p.65)
Bridge to Evening Island.

Fuji 617, 90mm lens, Fuji Velvia 100, f/32.

JOHANNA PARKIN (p.72)
Wine bouquet.

Sinar F2, Fuji Velvia 100.
I love to create shapes out of shapes, objects created out of their own essence, making an image that has more than one facet to it. In this case I wanted to make a fresh, bold, vivid image which is as full of summer, vitality and crisp colourful delicacy as the essence of what makes the image up.

BAPI CHAKRABORTY (p.68)
Tomatoes with attitude.

Canon EOS 40D.
This is heavily altered in terms of tone, but not shape; nothing needed to be plumped up. Dodging and burning was carried out in Photoshop to emphasise shape and texture.

JO HOLDING (p.73)
Mr McGregor's garden.

Canon EOS 40D, Canon 50mm f/1.4 USM lens, f/2.8.
I took this image at dawn to capture the dew on the lettuce, glistening in their regimented rows. The mist began to clear as the sun broke through, giving a narrow opportunity to take the photograph before the light quality changed into bright sunshine.

DEE FISH (p.69)
Freshly picked sweet basil leaves (Basilicum).

Epson Perfection 2480 Photo flatbed scanner.

JONATHAN BUCKLEY (p.74)
Sarah Raven holding a container of harvested forced chicory 'Witloof' and 'Rossa di Treviso'.

Kodak DCS, 105mm lens.
Cropping tightly to eliminate any other background made a simpler, more graphic image.

JONATHAN BUCKLEY (p.75)
Stripping redcurrants with a fork.

Canon EOS 5D, 200mm lens, 1/180sec, f5.6.
I had to use a shutter speed fast enough to capture the moment while also leaving a blur to preserve the sense of movement. This meant a wide aperture, which helped to draw the eye to the centre of the action. Timing was critical and it took a lot of attempts before we got a result we were happy with.

ANDY PHILLIPSON (p.82)
Enoki mushrooms.

Canon EOS 5D, Canon 180mm macro f/3.5 lens with 2x extender, ISO 125, f/22 at 1/4sec.
With a slow shutter speed and ground-level viewpoint, this shot became an exercise in both patience and tripod technique. I shot at several apertures but preferred the increased depth of field at f/22.

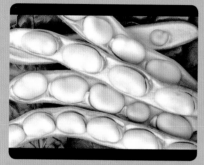

WILLIAM BROAD (p.78)
Broad beans.

Fujifilm FinePix S5700 set to macro.
The beans were freshly picked from my Aunt's garden, split with a razor blade then photographed from above against several different backgrounds and in a variety of arrangements.

DAVID MAITLAND (p.83)
Velvet shank fungus (*Flammulina velutipes*).

Canon EOS-1Ds Mk II.
This clump was at about chest height on the tree. I wanted an interesting angle to emphasise the gill structure, so crouched down beneath to look up into the canopy for a view from below. This also places the fungus in its habitat.

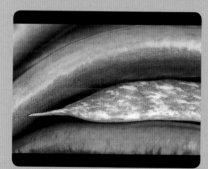

JO WHITWORTH (p.79)
Aubergines 'Farmer's Long' with borlotto bean 'Firetongue'.

Nikon D200, 105mm macro lens, f/5.6.

GARY ROGERS (p.84)
The gourd tunnel.

Nikon F3, AF-S Nikkor 17-35mm zoom lens, Fuji Velvia, f/16.

PAUL DEBOIS (p.80)
Pumpkins and squashes.

Kodak Pro/SLRc, Sigma 105mm macro lens, f/20.
The major decision was the type of lighting: tungsten or flash. I felt tungsten would be more suitable as it is warm when used with daylight film or daylight settings on a digital camera. But I also shot some with flash, and this image was the result.

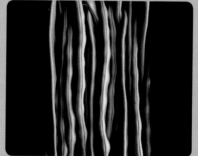

JOHANNA PARKIN (p.85)
Runner beans.

Sinar, 150mm Sinaron lens, Fuji Velvia 100.
The contours of the beans' edges shone beautifully in the light, so I wanted to make a graphic and linear shot that was slightly abstract, while retaining the honest organic naturalness inherent to these long, striking vegetables.

JOE FAIRS (p.81)
Fallen apples.

Canon EOS-1Ds, 80-200mm lens, f/8. Red adjusted using the selective colour adjustment tool in Photoshop.
The low angle, along with a telephoto lens, helped to bring the apples together. I don't remember placing them for composition. If I had, I think you would have been able to see footprints.

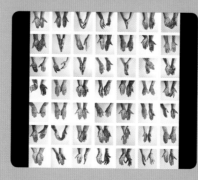

PAUL DEBOIS (pp.88–89)
43 gardeners' hands.

Canon EOS 5D Mk II, 105mm Sigma Macro and 85mm Canon lenses.
Each gardener was in a different location. Using a white background gave consistency. Lighting had to be identical. One flash was used with a reflector in the same set-up throughout. This meant I could work indoors or outdoors depending on the weather.

MAGGIE LAMBERT (p.90)
Rustic retreat.

Panasonic Lumix DMC-FZ5, f/3.2.
My position had to be chosen with care so it would not be visible in the reflection. A head-on view was necessary to preserve the pattern created by the windows.

ADRIENNE BROWN (p.95)
Gardening Boss.

Panasonic Lumix DMC-LX2, Leica DC Vario-Elmarit lens.
I decided to take the photograph from above to record as much information as possible and create a sense of distance. I liked the way the window framed the picture, and the extra interest created by the bottles and guitar head.

KEVIN COZMA (p.91)
Promenade.

Nikon D200, Sigma 10-20mm lens, f/5.6.
The most important detail is the use of a star-cross filter to achieve the twinkle in the lights. I also used a tripod and a shutter speed of 0.8sec, and an off-camera flash with a small softbox in rear curtain sync mode.

DAVID THURSTON (pp.96–97)
Nasturtiums.

Canon EOS 5, Canon EF 20-35mm L lens, Fuji Provia, f/8.
Fortunately, although it was a sunny day, the garden was in shadow. If it had been in direct sunlight, the colour would have been desaturated and the contrast of highlight and shadow would have been too severe for a good shot.

ANNIE WILLIAMS (p.92)
Elsie in her garden.

Canon EOS 20D, Sigma 70-200mm DG Macro HSM lens, f/2.8.
I spent a couple of hours in the garden taking photographs of flowers as Elsie was weeding, and just managed to catch this shot as she turned to me and smiled.

DAVID THURSTON (p.98)
Gates of Eden.

Canon EOS 5, Canon 28-105mm f/3.4-4.5 EF lens, Fuji Provia, f/11.
A straightforward photo opportunity. I was taking pictures when the owner appeared. She was happy to be photographed, too, although we could not communicate verbally because of the language barrier.

KEVIN COZMA (p.93)
Nature Girl.

Nikon D200, Sigma 10-20mm lens, f/5.6.
I manually exposed for the bottom of the leaves as I wanted them to be bright and alive. I use a Nikon Sb800 flash on-camera with a warming gel, and a mini softbox mounted on it. This exposed my daughter correctly and evenly, after I used flash value compensation exposed for her face.

SONIA QUINLAN (p.99)
On my own.

Olympus Camedia X-2.
The winding path draws the eye into the distance and invites the viewer to participate in my son's exploration.

LIZ EDDISON (p.94)
Jim Keeling at work.

Canon EOS-1Ds Mk II, Canon 28-135mm lens, f/7.1.
The low sunlight came through the window in shafts while I photographed Jim, which did much to enhance the beautiful, muted colour palette.

ANNE GILBERT (p.100)
Running from the rain.

Nikon D300, Nikon 18-135mm f/3.5-5.6 AF-S lens, f/20.
This shot was taken with the assistance of a tripod and a slow exposure (1/4sec) to capture motion blur.

SARAH WENBAN (p.101)
Rumi.

Olympus OM2, Zuiko 50mm lens, Kodak BW 400CN, f/1.8.
As this picture was taken in a fleeting second (there was no way this active toddler would keep still) I shot purely on instinct.

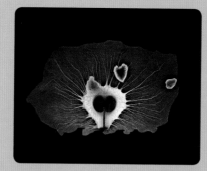

CEDRIC BREGNARD (p.108)
Sorrel and monkey's-comb seeds.

Phase One P45+, Mamiya 80mm lens, f/22.
I created a combination of positive and negative images of the seed in order to give the illusion of light passing through the grain of the wing.

JULIETTE WILES (p.102)
A break from the classroom.

Ricoh KR-10, 80-200mm lens, Fuji Velvia 50, f/8.
This was one of those spur-of-the-moment shots taken in seconds. I had been photographing the plants and had moved away to people-watch. As luck would have it, this little group of schoolchildren took my place and the shot just presented itself.

MARY SUTTON (p.109)
Poppy unfolding.

Olympus E3, Sigma 150mm macro lens, f/2.8.
The poppy moved a little, so I used a clamp attached to my tripod to hold it steady. A reflector created shade in order to maximise the tonal variation. By using a wide aperture I was able to achieve softness, yet retain some essential detail.

GERALD MAJUMDAR (p.103)
Tim.

Canon EOS 40D, Canon EF 24-70mm f/2.8 L lens, f/4.
I was chatting to Tim about his garden while taking several photographs. The day was quite overcast so I used ISO 320 and a zoom lens for different compositions.

JACKY PARKER (p.112)
A splash of spring colour.

Nikon D200, Nikkor 105mm micro VR lens, f/4.
I wanted to focus on the delicate little stamens of this flower while blurring the colourful background. I set the camera to Aperture Priority and used natural light.

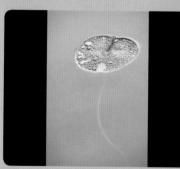

DEBORAH CASSO (p.106)
Lone lily pad.

Nikon D200, Nikkor 80-200mm f/2.8 lens, f/5.
I used a circular polarising filter with a modest degree of polarisation to cut down on the glare, but still leave a silvery sheen on the water.

NIGEL BURKITT (p.113)
Mount Cook lily (*Ranunculus lyallii*).

Canon EOS 40D, Canon EF-S 17-85mm lens, f/13, circular polariser.
I just had to include this stunning view of Mount Cook as a backdrop to my shot of the plant. I stopped down to f/13 so as to make the mountain itself out of focus but still recognisable.

KARIN GOLDBACH (p.107)
Romantic plants.

Nikon D200, Nikkor 105mm lens, f/3.

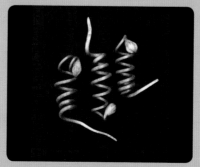

CAROLINE HYMAN (p.114)
Coiled cyclamen seeds.

Hasselblad, 135mm macro lens, Ilford HP5 Plus.
I used only natural light, and a piece of black velvet as a background.

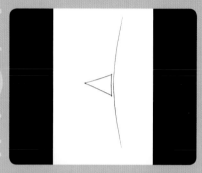

KEVIN HOWCHIN (p.115)
Reflected reed stems.

Nikon D300, Nikkor 70-300mm lens, ISO 200, 1/100sec at f/8.

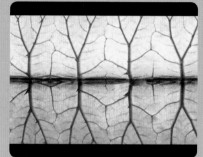

ANDY PHILLIPSON (p.126)
Victoria amazonica.

Canon EOS 5D, Canon 180mm Macro f/3.5 lens, ISO 200, 1/50sec at f/9.
The constraints of the water's edge and the low position of the pad meant that the photograph had to be taken handheld while I leant out over the water partly unsupported.

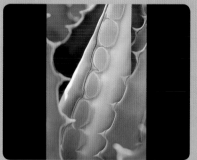

GEOFF DU FEU (p.118)
Agave utahensis.

Canon EOS 40D, 50mm macro lens, f/4.5.
Waiting for the leaf formation to be just right, with attractive framing and the light coming from the right direction, was a challenge that required many visits to this garden. It only finally came together in October, just before the seasonal closing.

DAVID SMITH (p.127)
Moss, *Bryum capillare.*

Olympus OM2, Vivitar 90mm macro lens, Fuji Sensia 100, f/32.
I chose this particular cluster because of the linear arrangement of the capsule stalks. I was able to coax the capsules themselves into the plane of focus by tweaking them gently between finger and thumb.

DONALD ROBINSON (p.119)
Asian lotus.

Canon Rebel, 400mm lens, f/8.

OLGA JONES (p.130)
Romantic tulips.

Nikon Coolpix 8800, ISO 50, 1/30sec at f/7.9.

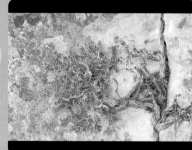

DAVID THURSTON (p.122)
Will to live.

Canon EOS 20D, Canon EF 28-105mm f3.5-4.5 lens.
The subject on the ground was in full sun. Long, strong shadows were a distraction to the form of the branches and leaves of the bush, and also created too much contrast. I removed my shirt and my wife held it in position, where it shaded the scene.

WILLIAM PIERSON (p.131)
Bougainvillea with blue wall.

Canon G10.
Once I saw the image, I moved quickly so as not to lose the light. Once on the scene, I went down on one knee to frame the bougainvillea in the window with the metal framework, to complete the composition.

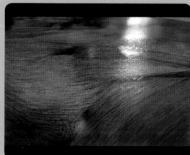

SEISHI NAGATSUKA (p.123)
Water plant.

Handmade 8x10in camera, 420mm Fujinon lens, f/22, flash.

NOEL BROWNE (p.134)
Autumn.

Canon EOS 30D, Canon 10-22mm lens, ISO 100, one second at f/16.
I wanted to get down to the toadstools' level and exaggerate the perspective by using a very wideangle lens. It was important for them all to be in focus.

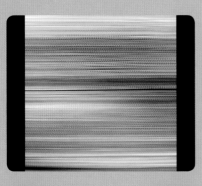

BRENTON WEST (p.135)
Phormium.

Canon EOS 5D, 24-105mm lens, ISO 100, 1/320sec at f/5.6.

RAOUL SLATER (p.142)
Jacaranda (*Jacaranda mimosifolia*).

Canon EOS 30D, Canon 300mm f2.8 L IS lens, f/2.8.

STEFFIE SHIELDS (p.136)
Blanket stitch.

Nikon 200D, Nikkor DX 18-70mm lens, ISO 100, 1/80sec at f/4.5.
I shot on automatic. A narrow depth of field threw the background out of focus. I took several shots, choosing different focus points on the encrusted edges. This worked best because the red leaf had both the brightest colour and strongest position.

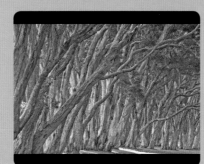

GARY STEER (p.143)
Evening paperbarks.

Canon EOS 10D, Canon EF 35-350mm zoom lens, one second at f/19.
Because of the diminishing light, I set the camera on a tripod to allow a slow shutter speed, and to maintain a large depth of field.

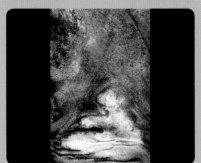

NORLE COLUSSI (p.137)
The art of imperfection III.

Canon EOS 30E, Canon EF 28-105mm f/3.5-4.5 II USM lens at 105mm setting, Kodak E100VS, f/22.
I didn't have a macro lens, so I was limited as to how close I could get. It was hard to fill the frame with my zoom lens's closest distance of 0.5m. I had to fine-tune camera position to avoid sky or grass on the corners.

GARY RAYNER (p.144)
Old tree detail II.

Canon EOS 3, Canon EF 24-85mm USM lens, Fuji Sensia 100.

DENNIS FRATES (p.140)
Lone fall tree.

Canon EOS-1Ds Mk II, Canon 70-200mm f/2.8 L lens, f/14.
The light around the tree was enhanced using Levels in Photoshop.

KIMBERLY BARDOEL (p.145)
Afloat in the branches.

Nikon D50, Nikkor 70-300mm, f/11.
I stood on the boardwalk observing the bog and looking for a subject. When I noticed this lone leaf there was a faint outline of the branches, but I knew if I waited for the light the reflection would brighten. I composed the picture and, when the sky opened, it created a depth to the reflection.

CHRIS HUMPHREYS (p.141)
Enclosure.

Nikon D80, 18-135mm f/3.5-5.6 lens, f/8.
A higher ISO (500) and a wider aperture was needed as light was limited and I was at the far end of the zoom. I sat on the road, locking the camera to my knees with my elbows to steady it. I needed a full stop of exposure compensation as the camera's metering was over-exposing due to the dark foliage.

ADAM GIBBS (p.148)
Roots (*Pinus ponderosa*),
The western yellow pine.

Toho-Shimo FC45X camera.

TECHNICAL INFORMATION

PETE BRIDGWOOD (p.149)
Lochan na h'Achlaise by torchlight.

Canon EOS-1Ds Mk III, Canon EF 17-40mm f/4 L USM lens, ISO 100, two minutes at f/10. White balancing to correct the tungsten (torch-lit) colour temperature of the island has resulted in some wonderful super-saturation of the twilight blues.

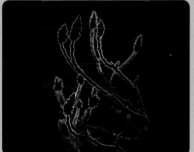

TONY JONES (p.150)
Rhus typhina 'Dissecta'.

Sony A100, 55-200mm zoom lens, f/8. I was inspired by the tree's structure in the *contre-jour* light. The maroon heads on the branches were a finishing touch of colour. I underexposed the photo considerably to achieve the dark, backlit effect.

TOM WUNDRAK (p.151)
Arboreum XVI.

Nikon DSLR, 20-35mm lens, f/2.8.

RICHARD LOADER (p.152)
Weeping spruce (*Picea breweriana*) in autumn.

Canon EOS 40D, Canon 35-350mm lens, f/6.3. Light levels were very low. I was concerned about getting a sharp image because the foliage was moving in the wind. The saturation was raised to enhance the colours of the leaves in the background and a little fill light was used to lift the brightness.

PAUL DEBOIS (p.153)
Junction 6 no.1.

Kodak Pro/SLRc, 105mm Sigma macro lens, f/16-f/22. As I didn't want to create a 'perfect' panoramic, most of the shots were handheld so there would always be an overlap or random join. The traffic shots were taken on a tripod so a slower shutter speed could be used to create blur.

MICHA PAWLITZKI (p.156)
American aspen trees (*Populus tremuloides*) in first light.

Rollei 6008 integral, Distagon 50mm f/4 lens, Fuji Velvia 100, 1/4sec.

CHRISTINA BOLLEN/ GAP PHOTOS (p.157)
Frosted fallen leaves.

Canon EOS-1Ds Mk III, EF 100mm f/2.8 lens, f/14. The light levels were low under the tree and, with a shutter speed of 1/8 sec, I used a tripod and cable release to eliminate camera shake.

ADAM TRIGG (p.158)
Shadows in the evening light.

Nikon D200, Nikon 18-200mm f3.5-5.6 DX lens, f/10. A small 'untidy' branch was removed as it compromised the composition slightly.

PETER O'HARE (p.159)
On fire.

Canon EOS 350D, 70-300mm lens, f/5.6. Contrast and brightness adjusted in Adobe Photoshop.

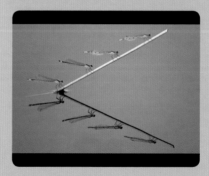

COLIN VARNDELL (p.162)
Damselflies on garden pond.

Nikon D2X, Nikkor 200mm macro lens, f/5.6. The wide aperture was selected to ensure the background was soft. But the resulting shallow depth of field necessitates being perfectly parallel with the subject.

MAGDALENA WASICZEK (p.163)
Summer shower.

Nikon D80, Helios 77 50mm f/1.8 lens plus 0.8mm macro ring, ISO 125, 1/200sec at f/5.6.

OLEGAS KURASOVAS (p.168)
Diamonds on 'fur'.

Canon EOS 20D, Canon 100mm f/2.8 macro lens, f/11.
It was impossible to get good depth of field at high magnification, so I took nine shots with different focus plane and then combined them in Photoshop.

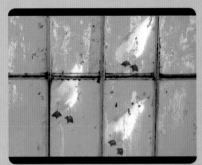

JOHN PENBERTHY (p.164)
Gulls on glasshouse roof.

Panasonic FZ20, Leica 10x zoom, 1/125sec at f/4.
I laid the camera on its back and used the balustrade to steady it, making several exposures until I was happy with the exposure and balance.

ALISTAIR CAMPBELL (p.169)
Patience.

Canon EOS 30D, Canon MPE-65 macro lens, f/6.3.
This is a composite of two separate images taken at different focal points but the same point of view, that were layered together in Photoshop CS3. This technique is called focus stacking. I used this to increase depth of field without sacrificing the sharpness.

RAOUL SLATER (p.165)
Wattlebird on forest grass tree (*Xanthorrhoea latifolia*).

Canon EOS 30D, Canon 100-400mm 'L' lens, f/11.
The photo was shot in colour. I then used the blue channel in channel mixer (Photoshop) to turn the sky pure white. A little selective burning and dodging highlighted the texture on the spikes and bird.

ALBERT ROBB (p.170)
Crow on nest.

Canon EOS 5D, Canon 70-300mm zoom lens, f/2.8.
The shot was made up of two images, both of which were taken on the same shoot. The crow and the nest were added to the main background image, because the trees needed a point of focus. They slotted together well.

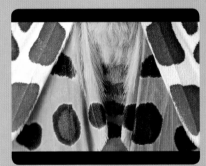

PAUL KEENE (p.166)
Garden tiger moth (*Arctia caja*) close-up.

Canon EOS 30D, Canon 100mm f/2.8 macro lens, 0.8sec at f/16.
I found a woolly bear caterpillar near to where I live and fed it with nettles until it pupated. When the moth emerged it was in pristine condition and I took several photographs before letting it go that night.

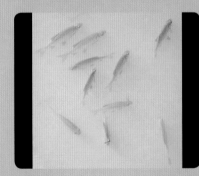

CHRISTINE WHATLEY (p.171)
Fish at Sir Harold Hillier Gardens.

Nikon Coolpix E4300, f/4.9.
It was an unexpected visit without my SLR camera, which invariably results in the best photo opportunities!

SARAH-FIONA HELME (p.167)
Summer stripes.

Canon EOS 40D, 180mm macro lens, f/4.5.
I took some shots at ground level but I wanted to show the full complement of stripes, so I then decided to take the shot from directly above to create a bold and colourful image.

FERGUS GILL (p.174)
Goldfinch (*Carduelis carduelis*) feeding on a teasel (*Dipsacus fullonum*).

Nikon D200, 300mm f/2.8 lens, f/2.8.
I rested my camera on a beanbag, which gave me a steady base and also concealed me from the goldfinches. It's critical on such cold days they aren't disturbed, as they need to eat as much as possible to survive.

COLIN VARNDELL (p.175)
Young starlings fighting.

Nikon D2X, Nikkor 500mm lens, f/8.
A tripod was used to set the lens in the correct position to capture the birds just above the bird table.

JANE LEWIS (p.181)
Poised for action.

Nikon D40, AF-S Nikkor 55-200mm lens, automatic.

CHRIS MINIHANE (p.176)
Bug on thistle bush.

Nikon D200.
This photo was taken in strong wind conditions on the top of a one-metre-tall thistle bush.

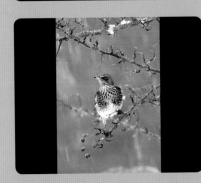

CRAIG CHURCHILL (p.182)
Fieldfare in the snow.

Nikon D2X, Nikon 500mm f/4 AF-S II lens, f/6.7.
The shot was taken from my vehicle using a beanbag for support on the window ledge. I sat and waited until the fieldfare returned and perched on an exposed branch to make the most of the falling snow.

KRZYSZTOF TRUSZ (p.177)
Bumblebee in the grass.

Panasonic FZ-20, f/6.5.

VALERIE McANINCH (p.183)
New snow.

Canon EOS Digital Rebel XT, Canon 300mm EF lens, f/5.
I knew with low light and a long lens that I would have to sacrifice depth of field, so I focused on getting the closest bird as sharp as possible. I didn't want too much blur in the falling snowflakes, so I used a 1/500sec shutter speed.

JASON SMALLEY (pp.178–179)
Wings of newly emerged dragonfly.

Canon EOS-1Ds Mk II, 100mm macro lens, f/4.5.

KAT WATERS (pp.186–187)
Purple haze.

Nikon D60, 18-55mm lens at 55mm setting, f/5.6.
I used Adobe Photoshop to apply radial blur in zoom mode.

PATRICIA FENN (p.180)
Smiling tree frog on cloche.

Canon EOS-1D Mk II, Canon 100mm macro lens, ISO 400, f/6.4.
I wanted to show the suckers on the frog's toes, as well as the golden eye and smiley face, so I had a bit of crawling around to do to get them all in focus. I liked the straight lines of the cloche against the random pattern of the frog, and the light coming through.

DAZYL YOUNG (p.188)
A squirrel's gaze.

Nikon D50.
The squirrel kept appearing in the tree so I immediately set up my tripod and, after some time, it finally looked towards my camera.

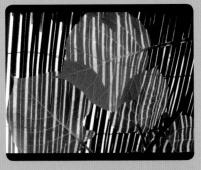

HANNAH BAYNE (p.189)
Kiwi tree (*Actinidia deliciosa*) in my garden.

Canon G9.

ESME MORISHIMA (p.190)
Bonjour.

Nikon D40, 18-55mm lens.
To achieve this depth of field, I had to have a very wide aperture. Luckily, snails don't require very fast shutter speeds.

JOE GOLDMAN (p.191)
Autumn bench.

Nikon D70, Nikkor 18-70mm lens, f/5.6.
I used aperture priority and a tripod so the shutter speed would not be an issue. I increased the saturation slightly and added a vignette and desaturated some areas in Photoshop.

JACK ASHWORTH (p.192)
Maggot's eye view.

Fujifilm FinePix S8000fd, f/3.5.

HOLLY HOLSTON (p.193)
Moss.

Kodak Easyshare M853.

BEN MIESZKOWSKI (p.194)
Eliot.

Fujifilm FinePix S5800, f/4.9.

JAMIE GOULD (p.195)
The smoking gardener.

Nikon D40X, Nikkor AF-S 18-70mm lens, 1/125sec at f/4.5.
I tried to take the picture before my granddad noticed me, so it would be as natural as possible. The file was desaturated to create a black and white image.

JAMIE UNWIN (p.196)
Chinese lantern *Physalis alkekengi* var. *franchetii*.

Sony A350, Sigma 70-300mm f/4-5.6 APO DG macro lens, f/7.1.
I set up my camera on a cold but sunny day in January at about midday, when the sun was coming right through the seedpods. I put my camera on a tripod and adjusted the focusing and aperture to get things just right.

BRIDIE HUSBAND (p.197)
Swallowtail caterpillar.

Canon EOS 400D, Canon 100-400mm f/4.5-5.6 L IS lens, f/5.7.

SAM ROWLEY (p.198)
Glowing leaves.

Nikon D200, Nikon 70-300mm f/4.5-5.6 VR lens, f/4.8.

TECHNICAL INFORMATION

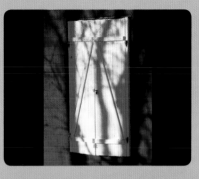

SAM ROWLEY (p.198)
Evening door.

Nikon D200, Nikon 70-300mm f/4.5-5.6 VR lens, f/4.8.

ISABEL GARBETT (p.203)
Autumn maple.

Nikon Coolpix.

SAM ROWLEY (p.199)
Yellowhammer prance.

Nikon D200, Nikon 70-300mm f/4.5-5.6 VR lens, f/5.6.
I used a wide aperture as I needed a fast shutter speed if I was to capture the bird's movement.

ROSIE TURNER (p.204)
Where my heart lies.

Fujifilm FinePix E900.
The photograph was converted to grayscale and the heart was selected and the colour changed to red.

BEN MIESZKOWSKI (p.200)
Sweet chestnuts.

Fujifilm FinePix S5800, f/3.5.

DOMINIC JONES (p.205)
Ray of dawn.

Canon EOS 400D, Canon EF-S 18-55mm f/3 5-5.6 lens, f/11.

PETER CURRY (p.201)
Tree reflection on path.

Panasonic Lumix.

KAT WATERS (p.202)
High and dry.

Olympus C-8080 WZ, 7.1-35.6mm lens at 23mm, f/3.2.
As I was taking this photo, I knew I would convert it to black and white. I wanted a shallow depth of field so that the somewhat messy background wouldn't detract from the main subject. The photo was desaturated and I applied split toning in Adobe Photoshop.

INDEX

INDEX

INDEX

The contact details for all of the photographers featured in this book, with the exception of Young Garden Photographer, can be found at the International Garden Photographer of the Year website, www.igpoty.com